# Praise for *Mission-C*

"I have been teaching and coaching leaders for nearly forty years. I consistently find that no matter how well they learn to lead their direct reports, they are often derailed because they neglect managing up and sideways. *Mission-Critical Leadership* gives substance to 360 perspective and development. The tips and examples will help you start implementing new ways of connecting and influencing today."

**Dr. Marcia Reynolds, internationally recognized leadership coach and author of *The Discomfort Zone: How Leaders Turn Difficult Conversations into Breakthroughs***

*"Mission-Critical Leadership* is the book for our times. Jon Lokhorst dives into the complexity and challenges facing businesses today and shares his practical, actionable roadmap for leadership success. Filled with real-world examples, contemporary research, straightforward how-tos, and insightful challenges, this book offers what leaders need to help their organizations, employees, and themselves reach their mission outcomes."

**Julie Winkle Giulioni, Co-Author, *Help Them Grow or Watch Them Go: Career Conversations Organizations Need and Employees Want***

"Jon shared the *Mission-Critical Leadership* framework with our team during a significant time of growth for our organization. Many of our managers and supervisors had little or no formal leadership training at that point. Jon inspired a

i

fresh understanding among our entire leadership team about what it takes to be an effective leader, not just a good boss. I highly recommend this book for all leaders who want to maximize their impact on the people they serve."

**Steve Gray, Founder and CEO, Family Innovations Inc.**

"Jon Lokhorst creates a whole new meaning to the phrase "all-around great leader." Today's leaders must be multi-directional and omnichannel, providing influence that is visionary, clear, and smart. His riveting stories, profound wisdom, and pragmatic takeaways make *Mission-Critical Leadership* a must-read for leaders committed to the success of their organizations."

**Chip R. Bell, author of *Inside Your Customer's Imagination***

"Jon's creative approach to the multiple facets of leadership is an essential read for anyone committed to improving their leadership skills. The complexities of leading during a pandemic have accentuated an even greater need for a new and innovative view of leadership. *Mission-Critical Leadership* provides just that by presenting leadership as a multi-directional process—an approach that will benefit both leaders and organizations."

**Ann Ownby Hicks, PhD, Dean, School of Business and Nonprofit Management, North Park University**

"Effective leadership in the 20th century was about DOING. That is no longer enough. We have learned that effective leadership in the 21st century is about BEING, specifically BEING someone that others want to follow. Unfortunately, recent events have left leaders feeling pressured to resort back to a focus on DOING and outcomes. *Mission-Critical Leadership* is a timely reminder that if leaders want to effectively navigate their increasingly complex environments, they must elevate their BEING. Let Jon Lokhorst be your guide in BEcoming a leader that can accelerate the realization of your mission-critical purpose."

**Ryan Gottfredson, PhD, author of the *Wall Street Journal* and *USA Today* best-seller, *Success Mindsets: The Key to Unlocking Greater Success in Your Life, Work, & Leadership***

THE INSIDE TRACK FOR ASCENDING LEADERS

# MISSION-CRITICAL
# LEADERSHIP

## HOW SMART MANAGERS LEAD
## WELL IN ALL DIRECTIONS

# JON LOKHORST

INDIE BOOKS
INTERNATIONAL·

The views and opinions in this book are those of the author at the time of writing this book and do not reflect the opinions of Indie Books International or its editors.

Neither the publisher nor the author is engaged in rendering legal, tax, or other professional services through this book. The information is for business education purposes only. If expert assistance is required, the services of appropriate professionals should be sought. The publisher and the author shall have neither liability nor responsibility to any person or entity with respect to any loss or damage caused directly or indirectly by the information in this publication.

Delta Sky Club™ is a trademark of Delta Air Lines, Inc.

RightPath® is a trademark of RightPath Resources, Inc.

GALLUP® and StrengthsFinder® are trademarks of Gallup, Inc.

Myers-Briggs Type Indicator® is a registered trademark of The Myers & Briggs Foundation.

Everything DiSC® is a registered trademark of John Wiley & Sons, Inc.

SpaceX® is a registered trademark of Space Exploration Technologies Corp.

Whenever just a first name is used in this book in a story, the story is based on a true story but the names and certain details have been changed to maintain confidentiality. The story is merely being used to illustrate a point. If the story is fictional, that is duly noted.

ISBN-13: 978-1-952233-57-9
Library of Congress Control Number: 2021905339r

Designed by Joni McPherson, mcphersongraphics.com

INDIE BOOKS INTERNATIONAL, INC®
2424 VISTA WAY, SUITE 316, OCEANSIDE, CA 92054

www.indiebooksintl.com

*This book is dedicated to Stefanie, John, Phil, and other ascending leaders who strive daily to lead well in all directions.*

# CONTENTS

# PREFACE

# The Lightning Speed Of Leadership

I will never forget the first Indie Family and Friends Forum I attended at the invitation of my publisher, Indie Books International. The event was held during the first weekend of March, 2020, in La Jolla, California. Our community of over sixty speakers, authors, and consultants gathered to learn how to deliver our best value to the people we serve.

There was talk of the coronavirus, which had been gaining attention in the news media in the week or two leading up to the event. The organizers equipped each goodie bag with a small bottle of hand sanitizer. Hugs and handshakes were discouraged. After each presentation, the microphone was cleaned with sanitizing wipes. Still, the virus seemed more like a nuisance than a threat.

That changed during my visit with a healthcare client in nearby San Diego the following Monday morning. As we concluded our tour of the campus, the executive director was met by one of his department leaders with an announcement from their headquarters.

"We've been told to close the campus to all nonessential visitors," he said.

"I assume I'd be defined as nonessential," I replied. "I guess it's time for me to leave for the airport."

After passing through security, I entered the Delta Sky Club to grab lunch and make a phone call prior to my flight. The expressions on the faces of patrons at the bar was one of fear, as their eyes were fixed on a large television screen. The stock market was down over 2,000 points.

"Houston, we have a problem," I thought, reckoning back to the famous words uttered by Tom Hanks's character, Commander Jim Lovell, in the movie *Apollo 13*.

I soon boarded my flight and promptly cleaned my seat, armrests, and table tray with a sanitizing wipe. I scooted closer to the window to keep my distance from the person in the middle seat. After takeoff, I looked down over Point Loma, wondering what was in store during the days ahead.

A few days later, the COVID-19 outbreak was declared a pandemic. Social distancing became a new way of life, as did shelter-in-place, whether voluntarily or by order of government officials. Professional and college sports paused, many businesses closed their doors (some for good), and organizations sent millions of workers home to work remotely. A Gartner survey showed that roughly half of all organizations had more than 80 percent of their employees working from home during the early days of the pandemic.[1]

As of this writing, the pandemic's new realities are still unfolding. After several weeks on high alert, the number of COVID-19 cases and deaths began to subside. The economy began to reopen, more gradually in some areas than others. Then, the number of COVID-19 cases started rising again, prompting government officials in many areas to pull back on their reopening plans.

In the meantime, many employers extended their work-from-home offerings. Twitter CEO Jack Dorsey and several other corporate leaders announced that their employees could choose to work from home forever.

By all indications, remote work is here to stay. Nearly half of CFOs surveyed by PwC plan to make remote work a permanent option for suitable roles in their organizations.[2] And most employees want more opportunities to work remotely. An IBM survey of 25,000 adults found that 54 percent of them would prefer to work remotely most of the time.[3]

> Remote work is just one of the rapidly changing conditions that will reshape the workplace.

Those who return to an office or working on-premises will face new protocols to protect against the spread of COVID-19 and potential future outbreaks. Ultimately, most organizations will become hybrids of remote and on-site work arrangements.

Beyond *where* the work is performed lie numerous changes in *how* this work is performed. The use of technology and the need to adapt to changing customer needs and preferences continue to accelerate.

As if leadership wasn't challenging enough before the pandemic, these new dynamics make it exponentially more challenging now. Leadership is changing at lightning speed and developing your leadership skills is mission critical.

# PART I

# UNDERSTANDING THE WHY

# CHAPTER 1

# Why It's Important To Lead Well In All Directions

Most people have never heard of Dorothy Vaughan. Even fewer people would know about Vaughan if not for her portrayal by the award-winning actress, Octavia Spencer, in the much-lauded 2016 film, *Hidden Figures*. Although she died in 2008, Vaughan stands out as an exemplary leader for us today.

Vaughan overcame gender and racial barriers to become a respected leader at NASA during the space race of the 1960s and 1970s. She began her career as a high school math teacher before joining the National Advisory Committee for Aeronautics (NACA, the predecessor to NASA) in 1943. She was a human computer, running complex mathematical calculations, mostly by hand, to provide data for NASA's scientists and engineers.

Vaughan was assigned to a unit called the West Area Computing Group, or West Computers, at Langley Research Center in Hampton, Virginia. As depicted in *Hidden Figures*, Vaughan and her colleagues worked in offices segregated from their white counterparts.

Vaughan was noticed for her technical expertise and, in 1949, she was promoted to a leadership role as acting supervisor of the West Computers. She was the first African American manager at NASA. It took several years, though, for her to get the "acting" part of her title dropped and officially become a supervisor. The movie depicts Vaughan's persistent, upward leadership toward her boss, to gain that recognition.

Vaughan stewarded her leadership role well. She advocated for increasing women's opportunities at the agency. She inspired her team to excel and worked to improve their working conditions. After learning the FORTRAN programming language, Vaughan taught it to many of her team members as they anticipated that electronic computers would soon perform calculations they had previously performed manually.[4]

Vaughan also leveraged her role to lead across the organization, collaborating with colleagues on other projects critical to the space race, such as the development of a handbook for using algebraic methods on calculating machines. Engineers sought her recommendations to match projects with the best workers for the job. She often used her influence to seek promotions and pay raises for deserving women in other departments.[5]

Amid all her accomplishments, Vaughan never lost sight of the mission for which she worked. She later described her work as being on "the cutting edge of something very exciting."[6] Vaughan and her team made critical contributions to United States space exploration. One could argue that without Vaughan's West Computers, NASA would never have achieved President John F. Kennedy's vision of landing a man on the moon.

What can you learn from Dorothy Vaughan's legacy?

The best leaders never lose sight of their mission.

They build positive working relationships while delivering crucially important results.

They lead well in all directions throughout their organizations.

They embody Mission-Critical Leadership.

## Mission-Critical Leadership: What Is It, And Why Is It What's Next?

In my work with leaders, I occasionally come across those who describe themselves as "old school." Often, these leaders include my peers from the baby boomer generation, who lament a perceived lack of work ethic among younger workers—millennials often being the target. They make statements such as, "When I was their age…" and continue with stories of walking a mile to school barefoot in five feet of snow. At least that's the version they use here in my home state of Minnesota.

Old-school thinking did not get us to the moon and back. Old-school leadership did not open the doors to space-related innovations like the Hubble Telescope and the International Space Station (ISS), and it won't produce the new ideas and innovation necessary to advance the workplace of the future.

Still, there are old-school leaders who hang onto a "command and control" style of leadership from decades ago. "These kids are so entitled," they might say about their younger workers. "Don't they realize they need to pay their dues like I did?" Or, "They need to stop complaining and just do their jobs." Then the old-school leaders wonder why younger workers are prone to change jobs more often.

Unfortunately, remnants of that stagnated mentality remain in the workplace. The mentality usually shows up in a lack of investment in leadership development. Many companies fear training their leaders, only to have them leave for other jobs.

This dilemma reminds me of a meme that made its way around social media a while ago:

> *CFO to CEO: What happens if we invest in developing our people and then they leave?*

> *CEO to CFO: What happens if we don't, and they stay?*

The CFO in this conversation doesn't realize that making the investment in people is one of the best ways to retain top talent.

> Talent retention and leadership development go hand in hand.

Both were rated as major concerns among human resource executives prior to the COVID-19 pandemic that was declared in early 2020. In surveys conducted between December, 2019 and January, 2020, more than half of 300 such executives surveyed said that retaining key talent was their biggest worry, followed by developing leaders and succession planning.[7]

## Then Came The Year 2020

The first two decades of the twenty-first century were replete with forces of rapid change. Technological advances brought the age of digitalization. These advances also broke down geographic barriers to make the marketplace an increasingly global one.

A new generation of workers, the millennials, entered the job market with a vigor to reshape the workplace. Companies such as Amazon, Apple, and Netflix transformed entire industries with new products, services, and business models.

2020 had such a nice ring to it, didn't it? The term "twenty-twenty vision" had a positive tone and was a great setup for leaders to set ambitious goals for the new year and decade ahead. In January, most parts of the economy were growing and the stock market was humming along with them.

It wasn't long, though, before a new word entered our vernacular: coronavirus. In the early days of the new year, the virus and the disease it caused, COVID-19, seemed obscure and far away, other than in parts of the world where it was spreading.

Within weeks, however, COVID-19 became a force to reckon with across the entire world. In early March, the outbreak was declared a pandemic. From a health perspective, there hadn't been anything like it since the 1918 Spanish flu pandemic killed an estimated 500 million people worldwide. The COVID-19 outbreak brought serious health ramifications across the globe—and the implications went far beyond health concerns.

The global economy took a sharp downward turn as businesses in many industries closed or cut back. Workplaces made abrupt shifts as shelter-in-place and work-from-home became a new normal. The crisis brought vast changes that will be long lasting and, in many cases, permanent.

## Your Best Leadership Is More Essential Than Ever

Our workplaces will never be the same. Organizational life is being reshaped more rapidly than any time in history. As a leader, you are leading in an environment that is increasingly volatile, uncertain, complex, and ambiguous (VUCA). This acronym was first used by the United States Army War College in 1987 to describe the rapidly changing world as the Cold War between the United States and Soviet

Union came to an end.[8] Subsequently, the concept has been used in many industries to describe the current challenges facing organizational leaders.

There is no better way to describe organizational life today. Our VUCA environment will stretch your leadership skills beyond what you can imagine. Are you ready to face the challenge?

## What Is Mission-Critical Leadership?

John Maxwell offers the simplest definition of leadership, boiled down to one word. "The true measure of leadership is influence—nothing more, nothing less," he writes in the widely read book, *The 21 Irrefutable Laws of Leadership*.[9] Maxwell's one-word description captures the key ingredient of leadership that compels people to behave or act in a certain way.

From an organizational perspective, it's crucial to incorporate a sense of action when defining leadership. Consider what psychologist, speaker, and author Dr. Henry Cloud says: "Leadership is basically getting from here to there."[10] The word "there" implies direction, vision, and goals. Cloud's paradigm is useful to describe leading at a macro level; for instance, when running an entire organization. It is also helpful at a micro level; for instance, when leading a team or project.

Cloud also emphasizes the two Rs of leadership: results and relationships.[11] It takes a mastery of both to be effective as a leader. Few leaders are evenly balanced between the two. Leaders who lean heavily toward results accomplish the goal, but if they're not self-aware, they risk devaluing or burning out their team members. Leaders who lean more heavily toward relationships can fall into the trap of people pleasing or overcollaborating, at the cost of progress toward the ultimate goal.

Effective leadership requires the right blend of effort toward results and relationships. It also requires a mindset of leading in all directions within one's organization.

> Most leadership development is focused on a singular direction within an organization—downstream in the hierarchy.

The best leaders, like Dorothy Vaughan, recognize the need to lead upward to their superiors and also across to their peers; and they start by leading themselves well.

Now that we have a better understanding of leadership in general, what do we mean by "Mission Critical"? The term conveys a focus on an organization's lifeblood and the factors that are essential for it to accomplish its mission and purpose. Impairment of those factors puts the organization at serious risk of decline or even survival.

At pivotal moments, when the stakes are high, leaders who focus on what's mission critical cut through the clutter, clear away distractions, and ensure their teams are devoted to what's truly essential. That's how Vaughan led her West Computers team.

Combining these concepts, I define Mission-Critical Leadership as:

> *Using influence to build relationships and deliver results in all directions within an organization, accelerating it faster and further toward its mission.*

Why would I open the book with a story about leadership from the United States space program? After all, I am not an astronaut, engineer, or scientist—nor do I play one on television. My interest in the space program dates back to my childhood, watching Neil Armstrong become the first human to set foot on the moon.

Ever since then, I have been fascinated by the high-risk, high-reward nature of space exploration. There is little to no margin for error when you lead in that environment. Your leadership could mean the difference between life and death. This mode of leading successfully in a high-risk environment is the epitome of Mission-Critical Leadership.

That's why this book includes space-related examples of leadership, along with stories from the marketplace and from my personal experience.

## Why Does Mission-Critical Leadership Matter?

Employee engagement in United States workplaces continues to flounder. In their last prepandemic survey, Gallup found that only 35 percent of workers were "highly involved in, enthusiastic about and committed to their work and workplace." Surprisingly, that was announced as good news, representing the highest level of engagement since Gallup began tracking the measure in 2000.[12] That's only about one-third of employees.

Thirteen percent of workers were actively disengaged—unhappy campers who at times sabotage their employers' efforts. That leaves slightly over one-half of workers in the middle, which Gallup refers to as "not engaged."[13] I call it the "meh" category: workers who show up, go through the motions, and collect a paycheck, with no additional effort.

Numerous studies show that employee engagement is a proven driver of positive business outcomes. Organizations with higher levels of employee engagement are more productive, profitable, and innovative than their competition. They achieve higher levels of customer satisfaction and even experience fewer workplace-related injuries.[14]

So what is the key driver of employee engagement? It's competent leadership. The relationship a worker has with his or her supervisor is paramount. Gallup's research indicates that managers account for at least 70 percent of employee engagement.[15]

The mantra is true: "Employees join organizations and leave bosses." Effective leadership is essential—up, down, and across the organizational chart.

Poor working relationships with coworkers are another major source of frustration among employees. 5 Dynamics, a provider of human performance systems, found that nearly 60 percent of employees work in teams to some degree. Of those, 41 percent mentioned they experience friction in working with colleagues, and about one-third of them have considered looking for another job due to a negative team environment.[16] Leading effectively among peers is the antidote to this frustration.

Some would argue the large number of unemployment claims during the pandemic diminish concerns about employee turnover. As a result, they suggest, there may be more candidates available than at any time since the Great Recession of 2007–2009. Remember, the economy recovered the number of jobs lost during the Great Recession within five years and experienced substantial job gains after that.[17]

As I write this chapter, economists are assessing what type of recovery will follow the pandemic-induced recession. How long it will take to return to near-full employment is a matter of debate. However, risking the loss of top people by betting on the ability to replace them adequately is short-sighted.

Furthermore, the baby boomer generation is rapidly exiting the workplace. The United States Census Bureau reports that about 10,000 baby boomers reach age sixty-five every day. By 2030, nearly all workers from the baby boomer generation will cross that threshold.[18]

Leadership development is a viable mission in and of itself. Organizations that make it a priority will have a solid pipeline of future leaders for years to come. Individuals who invest in their own leadership development make themselves viable candidates to advance to the next level of leadership within their organizations.

Getting astronauts to a destination off-planet is the kind of organizational mission that drives everybody to excel, and it offers a wealth of leadership examples that are inspiring, insightful, and illustrative of best practices. These lessons can be applied in organizations from nonprofits to educational institutions to corporations.

What's your mission?

# MISSION-CRITICAL TAKEAWAYS

1. Watch the movie *Hidden Figures*. Observe positive and negative leadership in action from each of the main characters.

---

2. Identify the VUCA forces most relevant to your industry and organization. Consider how those forces shape your need for leadership development.

---

3. Determine what "mission critical" means for leadership in your organization and your role in helping it move further and faster toward its mission.

---

# CHAPTER 2

# Leadership In Every Direction: The View From Space

On April 24, 1990, the Space Shuttle Discovery launched from Cape Canaveral. The shuttle deployed precious cargo to low-earth orbit: the Hubble Telescope. It was one of the largest and most expensive space telescopes ever constructed. Originally projected to cost 400 million dollars, the total investment in the project reached 4.7 billion dollars by the time the telescope was launched.

The Hubble Telescope was designed to capture high-resolution images of outer space made possible by the telescope's distance from light cast from Earth. However, scientists raised concerns just two months later when initial images from the Hubble came back with far less clarity than they had expected. Engineers tried several adjustments without success. The telescope could not achieve a clear focus and the image quality was less sharp than the scientists had expected.

The problem was diagnosed as spherical aberration, namely, the result of a seemingly small error by a technician involved in the fabrication of the telescope's primary mirror. The error caused a flaw in the curved shape of the nearly nine-foot-tall mirror. The curve was off by a mere fraction of the width of a human hair, but enough to substantially diminish the quality of images returned to Earth.

Much of the fix for the Hubble came from exploring a backup of the Wide Field and Planetary Camera, the device responsible for delivering high-definition images. The rest of the solution emerged from a far more unlikely source—an engineer's observation of plumbing fixtures while taking a shower in Germany.[19]

Eventually, these solutions were implemented by the crew of the space shuttle Endeavour in December 1993, salvaging the Hubble program and NASA's pride.

The Hubble mishap offers two important lessons. First, your best ideas show up in the shower. No kidding; this notion is supported by brain science. The combination of your relaxed state of mind and release of dopamine in your brain triggers creativity. So pay attention and consider keeping a notebook near your shower.[20]

The second lesson is that, whenever technical problems occur, look beyond the surface to find the underlying leadership problems at the root. That's what NASA's former Director of Astrophysics, Charlie Pellerin, did. He concluded that the problem with the Hubble "wasn't merely a technical failure. It was a leadership failure and a product of the culture surrounding the project."[21]

Pellerin said it was easy to blame the people doing the work. He wanted to understand why the fabrication error wasn't detected by someone among the smart people working on the project. Pellerin found that due to a variety of challenges, including being over budget, the staff were being "hammered on" to the point they didn't have time or inclination to look for any problems other than those most critical. Congressional hearings actually determined that leadership was at the center of the failure.

As in the Hubble example, nearly every issue in an organization stems from a leadership problem. Also, every big problem in an organization starts out as a small problem that someone in leadership failed to address. That is why it is crucial to sharpen your leadership skills continually as you advance within your organization.

## Why Should You Read This Book?

Have you ever felt stuck in your job? Perhaps you wanted to advance to the next level but felt a variety of forces holding you back?

Have you ever been frustrated with your boss? Like when you had good ideas that would benefit your organization, but you simply could not get your boss on board?

Have you ever experienced a lack of cooperation from peers at your same leadership level? Maybe you knew it would take a collaborative effort to accomplish an important project, but you got stiff-armed by the colleagues who could help you?

Have you ever wondered why the team you supervise fails to perform to your expectations? Do you wonder what gaps in your leadership skill set keep your team members from reaching their full potential?

If your answer to any of these questions is "Yes," this book is for you. The truth is, I have never met a leader who could answer "No" to these "Have you ever..." questions. Every leader, no matter how well-educated, experienced, and polished, has struggled at some point.

You may be struggling in one of these areas right now. Your frustration is building. You wonder if you are in the right job. It is tempting to return the last message you received from a professional search firm. Deep inside, though, you know jumping ship is not the answer.

> At your best moments, you know you have plenty of room to get better as a leader.

Reading this book and applying the principles you learn will help you do just that.

# An Introduction To Mission-Critical Leadership

Most leadership development focuses on a single direction: downstream in the organizational hierarchy. Yet most leaders I've met experience just as much, if not more, frustration from poor working relationships with their bosses or peers. The bottom line is that they don't understand their leadership role as it pertains to those relationships.

Mission-Critical Leadership requires that you lead well in all directions, not just downstream to those for whom you are "the boss." In Section II, you will gain insights on how the best leaders do just that. They effectively lead upward to their superiors, across among their peers, and down to their direct reports. In addition, as you will learn in chapter 3, all leadership begins with self-leadership.

(One important side note: the word "down" does *not* imply a lower value of those individuals; it is simply a reflection of the typical organization chart. This isn't the time or space to debate whether that model is archaic. In my view, it is a practical reality in most organizational design, even in places that claim to have a flat organizational structure. That's enough on this topic for now.)

## Overview Of The Mission-Critical Leadership Framework

**Leading yourself:** You can't lead others well unless you first learn how to lead yourself well. Expand your leadership capacity and prevent yourself from getting derailed by building a strong personal foundation. Without a strong foundation, buildings crack, crumble, and fall. The same is true of leadership. Once your foundation is in place, learn self-leadership strategies that will help you overcome the myriad of obstacles you will encounter on your leadership journey.

**Leading up:** This is the most counterintuitive form of leadership because your leadership flows against the current in a typical hierarchy. You will spend your entire career leading up to a boss. Most leaders who reach the pinnacle and become the "top dog" in their organizations still have someone to report to, if not to multiple superiors. The CEO or executive director is usually accountable to a board of directors or ownership group. Learning how to effectively lead your boss is essential to getting support and approval for your ideas. This skill is also crucial to earn opportunities for advancement. No one else has as much influence as your boss when it comes to your career trajectory.

**Leading across:** This is the most complex form of leadership. Neither you nor the person you are trying to lead have role power over the other. You might recall the statement, "You're not the boss of me." As a firstborn, I used it often during childhood. Well, this just doesn't work. Leading well horizontally requires a unique blend of trust and influence as you build productive working relationships with peer leaders within your organization. Doing so will get you noticed: leaders who break down silos to achieve the greater good enhance their chances for promotion.

**Leading down:** Leading in this direction is the most common view of leadership. This form of leadership is well understood because you have authority and role power over those you lead. If you rely on these dynamics, however, you will lose credibility with your team. Leaders who play the "boss card" too often eventually lose their right to lead. Instead, base your leadership style on influence, which will compel your team members to choose to follow your direction. Inspire their engagement with healthy communication, coaching, and recognition.

## Meet Your Leadership Coach

I describe my professional journey as a winding, jagged career path. It epitomizes Henry Cloud's depiction of leadership as getting from here to there. The road from "here to there" has brought many interesting twists and turns, with potholes and hazards along the way.

I went to college knowing that I was most interested in a business career. That interest soon narrowed to the accounting profession and I decided to become a certified public accountant (CPA).

I had my first job lined up before I graduated and I was sure about my career path: I would pass the CPA exam, work hard to move up the ranks in my firm, become a partner, grow my practice, and keep doing that until I reached age sixty, give or take a few years. I envisioned stepping out of the marketplace at that point to serve in a nonprofit role, perhaps related to my faith background.

Everything was going according to plan when the first major career disruption hit—nearly eighteen years into my career. The disruption came in the form of a sense of calling that led me to leave the CPA business for the faith-based, nonprofit sector much earlier than planned. That choice then led to fifteen years spread across four different organizations.

Over those years, I nurtured a growing interest in and passion for leadership and organizational development. As a CPA, I had a front-row seat to observe the impact of good leadership and healthy teams. I saw the difference between some organizations that would thrive and grow and others that struggled or even failed to survive. I noticed that some leaders' people loved working for them, while others were disdained. I had opportunity to practice my own leadership as I achieved my goal of becoming a partner, and eventually the managing partner, in my firm.

After that, my nonprofit experience gave me a view of leadership from the inside of an organization. Once again, I observed leaders who were effective—and, conversely, those who were not. I learned from my own experience as a leader, sometimes by finding what worked and other times by finding what didn't.

Through all of those career stops, I was a student of leadership. I attended numerous leadership conferences, read countless books and articles on the subject, and, once the podcast was invented, found ways to absorb insights from the best and brightest experts.

Eventually, that impulse to learn ignited the idea to make leadership development my final career, as I call it. I obtained a Master's in Organizational Leadership and earned a coaching certification, and then launched my own business. My goal? To help organizations develop leaders everyone wants to follow, build teams no one wants to leave, and deliver exceptional results. This book, *Mission-Critical Leadership*, is the result of my belief in John Maxwell's mantra, "Everything rises and falls on leadership."[22]

## Leadership During A Season Of Uninvited Disruption

I started writing this book just as the coronavirus pandemic began to rear its ugly head in the United States. The virus was only the start of a cascade of obstacles to my focus on the book. First, uncertainty created a fog over my schedule of speaking engagements at big events and conferences. The same fog gathered over smaller team facilitation engagements and training workshops. As reality set in, many of these engagements were canceled, postponed, or shifted to a virtual environment.

Like many other areas, my home state of Minnesota issued a shelter-at-home order to prevent the virus from spreading. Although I was accustomed to working from a home office, I was not accustomed to doing that every day, day in and day out, for long stretches of time. My wife was furloughed from her job and my daughter's family moved in with us while they were building a new home, filling the house with new activity and background noise. One day, as I was straining to concentrate on the book, a construction crew started tearing up the street in front of me, only a matter of steps from my office window.

On the positive side, my work-from-home experience helped to inform my perspective on leading in an increasingly remote work environment. I have included a special section on how to lead remote work teams effectively in chapter 6.

It seemed like every step forward on the book was met with a new barrier or setback. Just as I was regathering my energy and motivation, we unexpectedly had to put our dog to sleep. Sequoia had been my faithful companion and officemate, often laying by my feet with tacit encouragement for my deepest work. I discovered myself going through the stages of grief as I did my best to support my coaching clients in their leadership during the crisis.

I learned many of my clients were experiencing grief, too, due to multifaceted losses caused by the pandemic. There were the health problems and, in some cases, the loss of life caused by the virus. Other losses resulted from the cancelation of sports, after-school activities, and the shift to virtual classes, church services, meetings, and even family gatherings. Interestingly, the Harvard Business Review article, "That Discomfort You're Feeling is Grief," became the most downloaded article from hbr.org ever.[23]

My home state of Minnesota had just begun relaxing restrictions from the coronavirus when an even more serious tragedy struck. George Floyd, a forty-six-year-old African American man died in an encounter with a white Minneapolis police officer. That set off a wave of civil unrest that soon spread throughout the country.

While all of these factors made my work more difficult, they brought me back to my purpose for writing in the first place: to create better leaders and organizations. When I seriously considered putting the book off for a year, I recalled the graduate school assignment that sparked my interest in Mission-Critical Leadership.

## An Assignment That Became A Calling

As a final graduate school project, we were charged to create a personal leadership development plan that incorporated a variety of assessment tools. I decided to conduct a composite 360-degree feedback survey about my leadership in prior jobs. I reached out to over forty former bosses, peer leaders, and direct reports to learn more about their experience with me as a leader. Using an anonymous, online survey, I compiled the results and compared them across each type of working relationship.

I was pleased with the overall results, but surprised to find that my former direct reports rated me higher than either my former superiors or peers. The gap wasn't huge but wide enough to catch my attention. I realized that I could have done better at leading up and across—the two directions that are most overlooked in typical leadership development offerings. I suspected this might be the case with other leaders, which began my study and observation of what it means to lead well in all directions.

Soon thereafter, a client emailed me with the subject line, "A Favor." He was reaching out on short notice to ask for a presentation on leadership to a CPA group in downtown Chicago. My first response was, "Leadership. That's a mighty broad subject. Can you narrow that down to something more specific?"

"The group realizes it's a last-minute request," he replied. "Feel free to present a talk you've done in the past or choose a new topic that you would like to share."

I instantly recognized the opportunity to develop this concept of leading well in all directions. The content resonated with the CPAs, one of whom mentioned she had never heard leadership described from that perspective.

From there, I created what is now known as the Mission-Critical Leadership Experience, a day-long training event that brings together leaders from across all levels and departments within an organization.

> Not only do they learn the principles to lead well in all directions; they engage with the very people with whom they will experience that type of leadership.

The idea for this book emerged from one such experience. While meeting over lunch following a tour at a healthcare organization, Angela, the executive director, shared a mounting challenge. "Jon, I think you can help us," she said. "We continue to struggle with employee turnover. We've done a lot to get new staff in the front door, but I'm afraid they're just going to leave out the back door."

"What do you think is causing the turnover?" I asked, trying to get at the root cause.

"I don't think our supervisors know what it takes to be good leaders," she replied. "In fact, I don't think we always know what it takes to be a good leader at the executive level, either."

"What I do know," Angela continued, "is that turnover is costing us dearly. It's hurting us financially and creating a lot of wear and tear on our staff. Our number one goal has to be to reduce turnover. Do you have any ideas?"

I suggested the Mission-Critical Leadership Experience as a launch-point for a broader campaign to reduce turnover. I was convinced that helping everyone in a leadership role learn how to lead well in all directions would improve employee engagement and reduce turnover, along with other positive outcomes. Angela agreed and we scheduled the day-long training event.

Angela opened the day by sharing her number one goal for the year: to reduce turnover by ten percentage points. As we dug into the content, it was amazing to watch leaders from front-line supervisors to the executive team learn together and engage in ways to become better leaders.

At the end of the full-day workshop, Angela and I cofacilitated a brainstorming discussion to generate other ideas to reduce turnover. The organization implemented many of those ideas during its subsequent year-long campaign. Angela kept the campaign to reduce turnover in front of her leaders over the next year. Follow-up calls indicated they were making progress.

As I suggested at the beginning, Angela and I scheduled a follow-up meeting for one year after the launch experience. She was excited when I asked, "Well, now that it's been a year, how did you do?"

"We not only achieved our goal, we exceeded it!" Angela enthused. "The goal was to reduce our turnover by ten percentage points and we actually reduced it by fifteen points. In fact, we've gone from one of our organization's worst sites for turnover to one of the best. I can't describe how big the impact has been for our leadership team as well as our staff."

That is when I knew I had to find more ways to share the concept of leading well in all directions, not just downstream in the organizational hierarchy. I trust you will find this book to be a helpful tool for you to do just that—and to ascend as a leader within the organization you serve.

# MISSION-CRITICAL TAKEAWAYS

1. On a five-point scale (five meaning excellent and one for needs improvement), rate your current performance in each of the four directions of leadership introduced in this chapter.

2. For each of the four directions, identify situations that offer opportunities to apply what you're about to learn as you dive into each area of this book.

3. Reach out to past team members, supervisors, and coworkers for feedback on how they experienced your leadership. How could those insights be helpful as you read this book?

# PART II
# MASTERING THE
# HOW

# CHAPTER 3

# Leading Yourself

Have you heard of the astronaut who nearly drowned in space? Italian astronaut Luca Parmitano came within minutes of experiencing a tragic accident during a spacewalk on July 16, 2013. It was Parmitano's second spacewalk, only a week after he had become the first Italian astronaut to walk in space.

Parmitano and United States astronaut Chris Cassidy were on a planned six-and-one-half-hour spacewalk to perform maintenance and other tasks at the ISS. About thirty to forty-five minutes into the venture, Parmitano felt water in the back of his helmet. In response, mission controllers on the ground aborted the spacewalk and Cassidy and Parmitano began making their way back to the entrance.

Parmitano recounted his struggle to find his way back as his vision began to be obscured by the water in his helmet. As the sun set, he lost the ability to see more than a few inches in front of him while he tried to find his way to the airlock port to re-enter the space station, where Cassidy and the rest of the crew awaited him.

The water then began to fill the front of Parmitano's helmet, around his eyes, ears, nose, and part of his mouth. Officials later determined that one to one-and-one-half liters of water leaked into his spacesuit, most of it in his helmet. It got to the point where he wasn't sure if his next breath would take in air or liquid. He later said he "experienced what it's like to be a goldfish inside a fish bowl from the point of view of the goldfish."[24]

Parmitano's saving grace? His safety cable, which guided him back to the spacecraft where his teammates removed the helmet so he could breathe freely again.

At times, leadership feels like Parmitano's harrowing experience, walking around in a fishbowl with your eyes closed. You may not face life-or-death situations like this astronaut, but the leadership journey—while exciting—is fraught with danger.

You, too, need a safety cable to guide you. Self-leadership is your safety cable. In order to lead others well, you first need to lead yourself well. Otherwise, you will drown in the goldfish bowl.

## Put Your Own Mask On First

Grace was the top leader of a healthcare organization serving individuals with special needs. I could tell she was struggling when we met for a full-day VIP coaching session. Financial deficits were an added burden to an already heavy toll of leadership challenges wrought with staffing issues. Imminent burnout was apparent in her voice and demeanor as she and I explored questions about whether she should continue in the role.

"I don't think I can keep doing this much longer," Grace said. "I'm not sure if I'm the right person to lead the organization through these circumstances. The stress is getting worse and I'm more and more tempted to look at other job opportunities."

Grace's comment opened the door to an exploration of her leadership journey. "What led you to this organization and your current role?" I asked.

As Grace retraced the steps of her professional career, her voice gained energy. "I've always wanted to help other people," she said. "But dealing with all of the issues in my current job makes me wonder if I'm really doing much to help people."

Her response provoked me to ask Grace about the underlying sense of purpose she gained from her work. "What is it that gets you up in the morning and enables you to go to work every day?" I asked.

"The bottom line is, I care very deeply about our clients and the staff who take care of them," Grace said, her face brightening. "I'm doing everything I can to make life better for all of them. I guess even dealing with our financial issues is one way I can do that."

"I just wish I could handle the stress better," she continued. "I work so hard to take care of our people and the needs of our organization. But I don't always take very good care of myself."

Grace's plight was not unusual. Leaders often neglect to lead themselves well before leading others, which is the first fundamental tenet of Mission-Critical Leadership. Dee Hock, the former chairman of the VISA organization, once suggested that leaders spend 50 percent of their time working on self-leadership before leading in any other direction.[25]

What is self-leadership? Charles Manz, a leading researcher on the subject, defines it as "a self-influence process and set of strategies that address *what* is to be done and *why* as well as *how* it is to be done."[26]

Thankfully, Grace grabbed onto the importance of self-leadership. She invested time and energy to explore the steps outlined below as we worked together. There were many tough decisions along the way, but by being a better self-leader, Grace was able to lead her team through a challenging season to a better place.

## Beware Of Leadership Derailers

The first step to more effective self-leadership is to recognize the dire consequences of not leading yourself well.

Studies peg the leadership failure rate at 30 to 50 percent, meaning that up to half of leaders seriously underperform in their roles, to the point of being removed from them. Researchers use the term "derailer" to describe the reasons behind these failures.

Recent history is replete with high-profile CEOs who derailed, often with catastrophic economic results. The early 2000s brought us Kenneth Lay, Dennis Koslowski, and Bernie Ebbers, whose leadership failures led to the downfall of the once-profitable companies Enron, Tyco, and Worldcom, respectively. On their watches, the no-holds-barred pursuit of higher profits and increased stock prices led to accounting irregularities and other fraudulent practices.

While greed is a frequent leadership derailer, it's far from the only one. A study in the *International Journal of Economic and Financial Issues* identified five others:

- Interpersonal relationship problems
- Failure to build and lead a team
- Failure to meet business objectives
- Inability to change or adapt
- Overly narrow functional orientation[27]

Note that most of these derailers stem from a lack of what are commonly referred to as "soft skills," although I prefer the term "nontechnical skills." In fact, it's harder to develop nontechnical skills than it is technical skills. I've found this to be particularly true in the highly technically oriented industries I often work with, such as accountants, IT people, and healthcare professionals. Also note that the first two derailers on the list are caused by deficiencies on the relationships side of leadership.

Often, derailment results from a combination of these five factors. Consider Richard Fuld, who received the dubious honor of being rated number one on Portfolio's list of the worst American CEOs of all time.[28] Fuld was the CEO of investment banking powerhouse Lehman Brothers, a company synonymous with the collapse of the financial industry and start of the Great Recession in 2008. While Fuld has been criticized for strategic decisions, or a lack thereof, that led to his company's demise, his harsh management style has also been cited as a contributing factor. Fuld's intimidating presence even earned him the nickname, "The Gorilla."[29]

Travis Kalanick stands out as a more recent example of a business leader derailed by a lack of self-leadership. Imagine starting a company and nurturing it to a place of marketplace notoriety, only to be ousted as CEO of the company you founded! That's exactly what happened to Kalanick, cofounder of rideshare giant Uber.

Kalanick developed a reputation for treating people poorly and was recorded on video in a negative incident with one of his company's drivers. There were rampant complaints of harassment in the company that weren't sufficiently addressed. In early 2017, Kalanick was directed by Uber's board to take a leave of absence. Around that time, he admitted, "I must fundamentally change as a leader and grow up."[30] Unfortunately, it was too late—Kalanick was fired shortly thereafter.

It's easy to look with disdain at the likes of Lay, Fuld, and Kalanick, and declare, "That would never happen to me."

Don't speak too soon.

It's unlikely any of these leaders ever thought they would fall from grace either.

Consider the repercussions if you were to fail as a leader. What derailers would trigger that failure? Increase your self-awareness of the derailers that make you most vulnerable. Envision the circumstances that would allow them to raise their ugly heads. Like Grace, commit to developing the self-leadership that will enable you to withstand these challenges.

The next step to strengthen your self-leadership is to build a strong personal foundation.

## Build A Strong Personal Foundation

As Grace discovered, a strong foundation is essential to becoming a better self-leader and a better leader in general. You can't build a skyscraper on a foundation meant for a garage. Similarly, you can't sustain a successful leadership career without first building a solid personal foundation.

You need a strong foundation to withstand the many challenges, stresses, and strains you will encounter along your leadership journey. To build a strong foundation, you need clarity on the following questions:

Vision:     Where are you going?

Purpose:   Why is this destination important?

Mission:    What are you doing to get there?

Values:     How will you act along the way?

This section will guide you in answering each of these questions. One word of advice as you begin: don't let perfect become the enemy of good. It's easy to overthink this exercise and stall the process. Record what first comes to mind; then go back later to tidy up the wording. If you come up with a catchy saying, great. However, it's more important to discover the core elements that will guide your leadership journey.

## Vision: Where Are You Going?

The late Baseball Hall-of-Famer Yogi Berra was as famous for his misuse of the English language as for his coaching career. One of my favorite Yogi-isms is "If you don't know where you are going, you'll end up someplace else."[31] Yogi was right. That's why you need vision. Without a clear vision, you can't define your goals; and your accomplishments may lead you down a road you don't really want to travel.

Vision answers the question, "Where are you going?" This question is just as critical for individual leaders as it is for organizations. The best organizations have a clear and compelling vision. So do the best leaders.

What makes a good vision statement? One leadership text defines it this way: "A concise statement or description of the direction in which an individual, group, or organization is headed."[32] Leadership expert Burt Nanus suggests that a vision statement should attract commitment, energize people, create meaning, and inspire excellence.[33] It's a compelling statement of the ideal destination you want to reach at some point down the road.

## An Exemplary Vision

One of the best vision statements of all time is a line in John F. Kennedy's address to a joint session of Congress on May 25, 1961. Known as the "Moon Shot" speech, you can easily find a recording on YouTube. Here's what JFK said: "I believe that this nation should commit itself to achieving the goal, before this decade is out, of landing a man on the moon and returning him safely to the earth."[34]

> Kennedy's simple but powerful statement galvanized not just NASA, but an entire nation, to achieve the vision. History confirms that it worked.

On July 20, 1969, astronaut Neil Armstrong became the first man on the moon. Four days later, he and his crew splashed down safely in the Pacific Ocean.

Unfortunately, Kennedy didn't live to see his vision become a reality, as he had been assassinated nearly six years earlier. The fact that NASA and the entire nation carried Kennedy's vision forward is a tribute to his leadership. A strong enough vision can outlive the leader who conceived it.

That's the power of vision.

Now it's your turn. What's your vision? Where are you going? As you write your personal vision statement, consider the following questions:

- Is it energizing and inspiring?
- Is it aspirational yet achievable?
- Does it create a sense of urgency?
- Does it compel you to excellence?
- Is it concise and memorable?

## Purpose: Why Is This Destination Important?

Now that you've clarified your vision, it's time to discover the purpose behind that vision. Purpose answers the question, "Why is this important?" Purpose reveals motivation and offers meaning. Viktor Frankl, a psychiatrist who survived three years in Nazi concentration camps, once said, "Ever more people today have the means to live, but no meaning to live for."[35]

Sad but true.

Most people go through the motions from day to day, lacking purpose. The best leaders, though, rise above the daily grind and seek to make a profound impact on those they lead.

They've come to grips with their "Big Why," their reason for getting up every morning to do the hard work of leadership.

Face it: the road to your vision is full of twists and turns, not to mention potholes at inopportune places. There are countless detours and ways to veer off course. It's tempting to give up. At times like these, you will lean on your purpose, or Big Why, to keep going. Here are some questions to help you discover and articulate your purpose:

- What makes your vision so important to you?

- Why is it essential that you reach your destination?

- What will your life be like if you do?

- What will it be like if you don't?

- How will your vision impact the people you lead?

- How can your vision motivate you to persevere when you are tempted to give up?

Wrestle with these questions. Record your thoughts and share them with a trusted friend, coach, or mentor. Your purpose may take shape as a single sentence, paragraph, or bullet point list of key words and phrases. Be creative. Find or create an image and post it in a place where you'll be reminded of your purpose often.

## Mission: What Are You Doing?

The opening scene in the original television series, *Mission Impossible*, was famous for a line that played on a reel-to-reel tape recorder. "Your mission, should you choose to accept it...," was the message that accompanied top-secret instructions for agent Jim Phelps and his team. The recording ended with the warning that their actions would be disavowed if they were captured or killed. Five seconds later, the tape self-destructed in a puff of smoke.

Your mission probably isn't as ominous or life-threatening as agent Phelps's missions were—but it's no less important. Your mission is the key to attaining your vision. Mission answers the question, "What are you doing to get there?" Because it involves action, your personal mission statement should include powerful verbs that reflect your vocation and relationships.

A popular *Fast Company* article featured the personal mission statements of top business leaders. One of my favorites came from Amanda Steinberg, founder of the personal finance site DailyWorth: "To use my gifts of intelligence, charisma, and serial optimism to cultivate the self-worth and net worth of women around the world."[36]

Steinberg's reference to her gifts makes the statement personal. Her reference to women clarifies the primary audience she serves. The statement is powerful and compelling, giving something to work for and aspire to. It's a vivid description that encompasses everything Steinberg does in her leadership role.

Once again, it's your turn. What are you doing to attain your vision? How would you describe the work that moves you closer to your ideal destination? Here are a few questions to guide your thinking:

- How will you achieve your vision?
- Who do you lead?
- What do you do for them?
- Why is that important?
- What is the unique role you play for those you serve?

As you did for your vision and purpose statements, explore these questions and write a brief statement. Keep it short and easy to remember. A short paragraph or a few sentences will suffice.

## Values: How Will You Act?

Congratulations! You're almost done designing your personal foundation. This final segment addresses your personal values, defined by self-leadership authors Andrew Bryant and Ana Kazan as "personal or shared enduring beliefs or ideals about what is good and desirable and what is not."[37]

Your values answer the question, "How will you act?" They are principles to guide your actions, filters through which to make decisions, and virtues to use in evaluating behavior. I encourage coaching clients to get beyond generic terminology that has become commonplace on corporate webpages that list values. For instance, honesty and integrity are important values, but the terms themselves are so widely used that their meaning is diminished.

Choose words or phrases that resonate with you and hold you to a higher standard. Limit yourself to five or six bullet points that reflect your top priorities, rather than trying to cover everything. The following questions may be useful as you define your values:

- What is important to you?

- What qualities and behaviors do you admire in other people?

- What qualities and behaviors do you admire about yourself?

- What principles guide your decisions?

- How do you want to be remembered?

Keep in mind, it's not enough to have values; you must live them out. I have a laminated card from a once-leading global company, whose values were Respect, Integrity, Communication, and Excellence. These values look great on paper but they didn't stop Enron from becoming one of the worst frauds in history. To avoid that trap, reflect on your values regularly. I have a reminder on my calendar to pause each week to ask myself if my actions, attitudes, and words reflect my values.

## Discover Your Unique Design For Leadership

Knowing your strengths and struggles is essential to leading yourself and others well. Self-awareness about your unique design leads to greater effectiveness and, at the same time, lessens the risk of derailing yourself as a leader.

Lead from your strengths. The strengths movement has gained momentum since the 2001 publication of Marcus Buckingham and Donald Clifton's book, *Now, Discover Your Strengths*. In 2018, the Gallup organization reported that about twenty million people had taken its StrengthsFinder assessment. Here's how Gallup defines a strength in *StrengthsFinder 2.0*: "the ability to consistently provide near-perfect performance."[38]

The premise behind leading from your strengths is simple.

> Tapping into the behaviors that come most naturally requires less thought and energy, allowing you to employ those talents more frequently and consistently.

For instance, my strength of focus enables me to set clear goals and priorities at both an individual and an organizational level. This focus also enables me to block out distractions and concentrate intensely on what's most important in terms of those goals and priorities. Doing so allows me to gain momentum on key results areas, which ties into another one of my strengths—as an achiever.

Knowing my strengths provides an awareness that my own work and that of the teams I lead will be very results-oriented. That's great for meeting deadlines, staying within budget, and getting things done. This knowledge informs my desire to take on initiatives with clear goals, objectives, and targets. Productivity and profitability are among the top business outcomes that come from that strengths-based approach to leadership.

Is it possible to employ your strengths too much? An overemphasis on strengths can have unintended consequences. As Jerry Mabe, founder and CEO of RightPath Resources, states "Strengths overdone are more often the greatest hindrance to a person's success."[39] Unfortunately, we don't always recognize when we cross the line into overplaying our strengths. This lack of awareness leads to what researchers Robert Kaiser and Darren Overfield call "lopsided leadership."[40]

When my strengths are overdone, there's too much focus on results, which can be very tiring for myself and those I lead. It's easy to overlook the human element, namely relationships and work-life tensions. Being too focused can also lead to tunnel vision or a reluctance to explore new alternatives or opportunities.

In the assessment tool Mabe developed, this dynamic is referred to as a struggle, as opposed to a weakness, or nontalent. For each strength identified by the RightPath instrument, potential struggles are presented.

Seeing these factors scored on a continuum highlights the strengths a person is most apt to overplay into a struggle. The RightPath profile characterizes the most extreme scores on the continuum as intensities, which my coaching clients find helpful to understand their leadership style and potential pitfalls better.

How well do you know your strengths and struggles? There are numerous assessment tools to help you understand your natural wiring, personality, and behavioral tendencies. Most involve an online questionnaire that quickly generates a report of your results. That's true of both the StrengthsFinder and RightPath profiles.

Other popular tools include the Myers-Briggs Type Indicator, Everything DiSC, and Enneagram. Many of these resources have been replicated with free online versions, although let the buyer—or user of free version—beware, as they don't typically have the same research validity as paid resources.

To get the best value from these tools, debrief your reports with a mentor, colleague, coach, or trained facilitator. There are often valuable insights hidden below the surface that you won't find on your own. Make the time and investment to understand your individual uniqueness and leverage it for better leadership.

## Employ Self-Leadership Strategies

I earlier referred to Charles Manz as a leading researcher on the topic of self-leadership. Along with two other leading researchers, Christopher Neck and Jeffery Houghton, he coauthored the classic text, *Self-Leadership: The Definitive Guide to Personal Excellence.* Their work chronicles a variety of strategies that help to develop and practice self-leadership. These strategies are broken into three categories and listed below.

**Behavior-focused strategies.** These strategies focus on changing or adding actions and habits that lead to more desirable behavior:

- Self-observation
- Self-goal setting
- Self-cueing
- Self-reward
- Self-punishment/correction

**Natural rewards strategies.** These strategies focus on the rewards inherent in an activity, such as the pleasure gained from it. For example, I experience a natural reward when using a coffee shop as my branch office, as I enjoy the smell and taste of the coffee, the buzz of white noise in the background, and the relaxing atmosphere.

**Constructive thought strategies.** These strategies focus on changing thinking patterns to be more positive and productive:

- Evaluating beliefs and assumptions
- Visualizing successful performance
- Self-talk[41]

While all of these strategies are worthy of additional study, I will focus on the one that comes up in almost every coaching or training session on self-leadership: self-talk.

Everyone engages in self-talk to some degree. It may be in your head, or it may come out while you're driving or in the shower. It may not be conscious, but it's there. The question is whether your self-talk is serving you well. Is it positive and helpful, or negative and destructive?

Characters from two well-known children's stories provide a contrast between the two types of self-talk.

My grandkids love *Winnie-the-Pooh* stories. One of the more loveable characters in these stories is Eeyore, the downtrodden donkey typically beset by unfortunate circumstances. Even the tone of Eeyore's voice reeks of negative self-talk. It also reveals a prevailing belief system that researchers characterize as pessimistic (versus optimistic) and obstacle thinking (rather than opportunity thinking).

No wonder Eeyore never seems to shake out of it. As Andrew Bryant and Ana Kazan put it, "Whether you are imagining good things or bad, you are setting up a self-fulfilling prophecy."[42]

Contrast Eeyore with the story of *The Little Engine That Could*. As the engine climbed a hill, it declared, "I think I can, I think I can, I think I can." And it did—the engine made it up the hill. Like these characters, every situation in life and leadership offers you the opportunity to choose your self-talk.

As I often ask coaching clients, who do you want to become, Eeyore or the little engine? How can you reframe your self-talk? How will you remind yourself to talk to yourself in more positive, confidence-building ways? It takes practice but having the following short phrases in your back pocket will help when crucial self-talk moments arise:

"I can do this. I got this."

"I'm going to be successful."

"I'm learning from this experience."

"I'm getting better at this."

Stephanie Wilson, one of the few African American women to fly in space, named self-talk as the greatest challenge she faced as a NASA astronaut:

> My greatest challenge is my own self talk and being very disciplined and methodical about putting it in perspective and proportion. That is a full-time job 24/7, so there's not a lot of bandwidth left to be distracted or deterred by the naysayers. When you recognize that your biggest obstacle is only yourself, suddenly stepping off the face of the earth doesn't seem all that daunting or overwhelming.[43]

Like Wilson, mastering your self-talk is crucial to leading yourself well, so that you can lead others well.

As you practice self-talk, you can use it to ensure you show up as your best self in every situation, which leads to our last fundamental self-leadership practice.

## Show Up As Your Best Self In Every Situation

Bill was at a crossroads. He had a good job as a financial analyst for a multinational company, but he wanted more. He wanted to advance into a leadership role. Imagine Bill's frustration as he watched several of his peers get promoted—and he did not. He was stuck when he came to me as his coach, asking what he could do to get promoted.

I asked Bill, "How do others in the workplace view you?"

"I'm known for quality work," he said. "My reports are accurate and always done on time. I get along well with my coworkers. I get good performance reviews." He then conceded it would take more than that to get the promotion he desired.

I suggested a new approach to Bill. "You need to rebrand yourself. Find ways to show up as your best self and deliver your best value every day. Show up as a leader."

I challenged Bill to come up with three words that describe him when he shows up that way. Three words that would remind him to show up as a leader, as his best self. Three words that would help him get noticed.

Bill was up to the challenge and said he would return to the next coaching call with his three words. Fast forward to our next session. Bill quickly jumped in. "Jon," he said, "I have my one word."

"One word?" I asked. "I suggested three words."

"Nope," Bill replied, "I narrowed it down to one." I was curious to see what he came up with. "Firestarter," Bill continued. "I want be known as a firestarter."

Now I was really curious. Remember, Bill was a financial analyst—not a role you would typically describe as a firestarter. So I asked Bill to explain.

"I can generate endless reports, data, and analyses," he said. "But that's not what will get me noticed. To stand out as a leader, I need to use this information to ask pertinent questions, start conversations, and share insights that will help our leaders manage the business better."

From there, we worked on a plan that would help Bill show up as a firestarter. He did it. He started showing up as a leader—he was his best self and delivered his best value.

It worked!

Within a few weeks, his superiors noticed a change in Bill. Shortly thereafter, he received the promotion that had eluded him in the past.

You may not achieve the same results Bill achieved. You may not be able to rebrand yourself in one word as he did. But choosing a three-word personal brand adds a memorable form of self-talk to your self-leadership strategies. This choice enables you to show up as a leader—your best self delivering your best value. Every time.

# MISSION-CRITICAL TAKEAWAYS

1. If you haven't already done so, schedule time to determine and write the four elements of your personal foundation (Vision, Purpose, Mission, and Values).

2. Once your personal foundation is in place, ask yourself daily, "What does my vision require of me today?"

3. Complete one of the suggested assessments or review one that you have done in the past. Identify the factors that have the most significant impact on how you function as a leader.

4. Monitor your self-talk over the next week. Keep a symbol in view, such as a picture of the little blue engine, to remind yourself of the importance of positive self-talk.

5. Determine the three words that describe you when you show up as your best self and deliver your best value as a leader. Use those words to create a daily affirmation.

# CHAPTER 4

## Leading Up

I t was a cool, crisp morning at Cape Canaveral on January 28, 1986. Millions of people across the world eagerly awaited the launch of STS-51-L, the Space Shuttle Challenger. Although this mission was the shuttle program's twenty-fifth, it was far from routine.

This time, the Challenger carried a thirty-seven-year-old teacher from Boston, Christa McAuliffe. She was chosen from more than 11,000 applicants for NASA's Teacher in Space program. Her presence on the Challenger added visibility to the launch that day, with thousands of schoolchildren watching on television.

While the rest of the world anticipated a successful launch, engineer Bob Ebeling sat nervously watching in a conference room at NASA Contractor Morton Thiokol's headquarters in Brigham City, Utah. The night before, Ebeling told his wife, Darlene, "It's going to blow up."[44]

Only seventy-three seconds after liftoff, Ebeling's worst fears became reality as the Challenger exploded and all seven crew members aboard were lost.

In one of their prelaunch meetings, Ebeling and four of his colleagues tried to stop the launch. They didn't trust that the rubber seals on the shuttle's booster rockets would seal properly on what would be the coldest launch day ever.

Unfortunately, Ebeling and his fellow engineers could not convince their superiors at Morton Thiokol and NASA officials to delay the launch until a warmer day. Ebeling, who retired shortly after the disaster, blamed himself for not stopping the mission, nearly until his dying day.

"I could have done more," he said as he watched replays of the explosion. "I should have done more." Ebeling later told a reporter that he wanted to ask God why he was chosen for the job. "Why me? You picked a loser."[45]

Ebeling finally came to peace with his actions after a National Public Radio interview on the thirtieth anniversary of the Challenger explosion. As Jim Sides, a public utility engineer, listened to the interview on his car radio, he was moved to action. He wrote a letter of encouragement to Ebeling.

The interviewer, Howard Berkes, was prompted to collect other words of encouragement. Ebeling's former boss responded, as did the retired NASA official who had rejected the recommendation to delay the launch thirty years earlier. Then-NASA administrator, Charles Bolden, made a statement honoring "those like Mr. Ebeling who have the courage to speak up so that our astronauts can safely carry out their missions."[46]

Within two months, Bob Ebeling died in peace at age eighty-nine.

Ebeling's experience highlights the steep challenge of leading up, as well as the drastic consequences when upward leadership is unsuccessful. As you will learn in this chapter, successful upward leadership is dependent on both sides to lead well.

## The Most Counterintuitive Form Of Leadership

"Seriously, I need to lead my boss?" she said.

It wasn't the first time a coaching client had asked me that question, nor would it be the last.

"Yes," I replied to Samantha, "the best leaders learn to lead their bosses. Only a few people get to be the top dog in their organization. Even then, most CEOs report to a board of directors. Imagine having twelve or fifteen bosses."

Samantha sighed at the very thought of that predicament.

"You will spend your entire career leading up," I continued. "At times, you will spend more time leading up to your superiors than you spend leading down to your team members."

"I've never thought of it that way," Samantha responded. "But you're right. I'll probably always have a boss to lead up to."

"What are some of the benefits of learning to lead up?" I asked.

"I guess it takes leadership to get my boss to listen to my ideas and approve my suggestions," she answered. "And learning how to lead up will be important for me to advance in my career." From there, Samantha identified several specific areas where she could practice upward leadership.

As Samantha discovered, leading up is the most counterintuitive form of leadership. Roles are reversed as the follower takes the lead over his or her superior. Leading up is a difficult skill to master, but one that's essential to building a productive relationship with your boss and advancing within your organization.

Your upward leadership skills are transferable, too. What you learn from leading your boss will make you a better leader in the other directions—across to your peers and downstream to your team members.

> In addition, you should create an environment where your team members are empowered to lead up to you.

Here are five ways to develop upward leadership skills.

## Build Unwavering Trust With Your Boss

Trust is paramount to productive working relationships. That's more true of your relationship with your boss than in any other relationship. Your boss needs to trust you to keep your word and follow through on your commitments. Leave no doubt that he or she can count on you. Proving reliable in small things leads to significant opportunities. To use a baseball analogy, you might think you need to hit home runs to impress your boss. Unfortunately, the best home run hitters typically strike out even more. Consistently hitting singles and doubles will build trust and confidence from your boss.

In his book, *How to Lead When You're Not in Charge*, Clay Scroggins writes, "To build trust, practice faithfulness. Nothing will win your boss over like selfless faithfulness over an extended period of time."[47]

Another way to build trust is always to support and never undermine your superior. It's easy to get caught up in negativity at the water cooler. Let's face it: all leaders have their flaws. Your boss may frustrate you more than anyone else in the workplace. That certainly has been true of my experience. Even my best bosses left me shaking my head at times.

Criticizing the boss around your coworkers will eventually leak out and it could even cost you a promotion down the road. When I facilitate the workshop version of this book, I ask if anyone has ever said an unkind word about their boss that later came back to haunt them. Nearly everyone in the group raises their hand. "Oh yeah," said Jane, a midlevel healthcare leader sitting at the front table in one session, visibly pained from the fallout she experienced.

The danger is not limited to the words you use. Even negative thoughts about your boss can erode trust in the relationship due to a phenomenon that psychologists call confirmation bias. You may have experienced this dynamic in other parts of your life. It's like the person who wants to buy a red Ford Mustang convertible. The more he thinks about the red Mustang, the more often he sees them on the road.

Similarly, the more you think about someone in critical terms, the more you look for behavior to confirm your conclusions about them. If you incessantly view your boss as a clueless, overbearing jerk, guess what? Your boss will become even more clueless and overbearing in your mind. It won't be long before these thoughts damage the working relationship with your boss.

Steer your words and thoughts to a more positive tone. Find your boss's positive qualities and leverage them to develop a healthy working relationship with him or her. Building unwavering trust will position you for more considerable influence and open a seat at the table for you to join higher-level discussions within your organization.

## Master Your Craft: Do Your Job Exceptionally Well

Joe served on a team I led during one season of my career. He was sincere, kind, and easy to get along with. People enjoyed working with him, both inside and outside of the organization. However, Joe was prone to errors and couldn't seem to shake his careless habits. As his boss, I was too often fixing simple mistakes to ensure his work got done correctly. Sadly, for Joe, he was unable to master his craft. His carelessness eventually cost him his job.

Do your job exceptionally well. You can't become a go-to person for your boss if he or she can't count on you to take care of your responsibilities. Complete your assignments on time and within budget. Be proactive in communicating when things start going off course. It's hard to secure the promotion you desire when you miss deadlines, exceed budget, or fail to communicate.

Make the decisions that are yours to make. Don't defer decisions to your boss unless truly necessary. If you get into that habit, your boss eventually feels like he or she is doing your work. It's almost impossible to advance if you can't make the decisions required at your level of responsibility. Seek clarity if you're unsure about decision-making authority; consider it practice in leading up.

> Master your craft by developing the core competencies essential to your job.

I often hear about younger leaders who complain that they're not being developed in their current position. Don't wait for your boss or your organization to develop you. Create your own professional development plan. Pursue training, coaching, and mentoring to fill gaps between your current skill level and what you need to excel. Read books and listen to podcasts that help you refine existing skills and learn new ones.

Look beyond your current position. Seek opportunities that will prepare you to move to the next level. Volunteer for stretch assignments that enable you to learn new skills or provide exposure to other areas of the business. For example, if you need to learn how to lead meetings, ask your boss if you can lead a portion of your next team meeting. Think at the next level up. Start thinking like your boss, and your boss's boss. Don't overstep your bounds, but show that you can take on greater responsibilities.

Finally, build your team. You have more responsibility to develop others as you advance professionally. Help your direct reports excel in their roles and prepare them for their next level. Strengthening your bench makes you more promotable, as your superiors see that others are ready to step up as you advance in the organization.

## Adapt Your Communication Style And Preferences

As a subordinate, it's up to you to learn your boss's communication style and adapt to his or her preferences. That starts with knowing his or her preferred tool for communication. Does he or she prefer email to an in-person conversation? Or an exchange of text messages to a phone call? One of my former bosses leveraged the company voicemail system to leave messages for his team throughout the day.

Often, your communication is most effective by combining the tools available to connect with your boss. Andre, an IT leader I coached, was frustrated with the lack of response to the emails he sent to his boss. I asked if his boss was more responsive to other vehicles for communication. After recalling that his text messages were usually answered promptly, Andre decided to notify his boss via text when a critical email was on its way.

Another communication-related question is how he or she prefers to receive information. How detail-oriented is your boss? Some bosses would rather have a high-level summary that cuts quickly to the bottom line. Others want the details to draw their own conclusions. Scott, a hospital CFO, has his team provide a bullet point summary of each report, along with the full document so he can dive into the details for more information if necessary. Remember, it's a lot easier to start with the summary and move into more detail than the other way around.

How frequently does your boss want to communicate with you? The answer may stem as much from personal preference as it does the nature of your position. At one point in my career, I transitioned from working for a boss with whom I had contact multiple times throughout the day to one I didn't have any contact with for several days. I often recommend that my coaching clients schedule a regular one-on-one check-in meeting with their bosses if they don't already have one. Use this meeting to ensure you get the communication you both need.

Finally, how does your boss prefer to receive bad news? Some bosses want the story behind it, as a way of warming up to the bad news. Others prefer to hear it straight up, without any sugarcoating or a lengthy explanation. If you're not sure about your boss, ask now. That knowledge will alleviate stress the next time you are the bearer of bad news. Also, be discerning about timing when you have to deliver bad news. Your boss may be preparing for an important client presentation or board meeting. Ill-timed bad news can be worse than the bad news itself.

## Advance Your Boss's Agenda

Have you ever been excited to successfully complete a project only to be disappointed by a lukewarm response from your boss? There's a good chance the project was more important to you than it was to him or her. It's like climbing a tall ladder to paint the peak of your house, only to discover you didn't move the ladder close enough to reach the peak!

To avoid a situation like this, seek clarity on your boss's top priorities and strive to execute on them. Those priorities may relate to important initiatives that flow from higher levels within the organization. By helping move them forward, you gain credibility and visibility, not only with your boss but his or her peers and superiors as well. That, in turn, positions you for future advancement opportunities within the firm.

You might find this challenging if your boss succumbs to the "flavor-of-the-month" tendency of many entrepreneurs. It can be difficult if your boss moves quickly from one initiative to the next big idea—while you are still trying to implement the old one. Kristy, a healthcare leader with a fast-moving boss, raised that challenge in one of our coaching sessions. We worked together to craft questions to ask her boss for guidance on prioritizing between multiple projects. One such question was, "How would you like me to allocate my time between these initiatives?" Another was, "Which of these priorities should command the most immediate attention on my part?"

Find ways to take things off your boss's plate. Don't wait for him or her to delegate tasks to you. Let your boss know you have the capacity to take on more work—first, be sure that's true, so you don't jeopardize the ability to do your job exceptionally well. When you lighten your boss's load, it enables him or her to focus on other challenges. It also shows that you're capable of performing at a higher level of responsibility. Consider the ripple effect as you encourage the same with your direct reports. Leaders at each level can then devote more attention to strategic priorities that move the organization forward.

When possible, go beyond the call of duty and ask if there's more you can do. Randy was a college student who worked between school years at one of the camps where I was director. He was typically the first one done as we assigned tasks at the end of a summer camp week. Instead of disappearing to do his own thing, however, Randy came back asking what more he could do to help the team. I wasn't surprised to later learn that Randy had earned the Servant Leadership Award from his university.

Here's one final aspect of helping to advance your boss's agenda.

> Partner with your boss in leading change. Research indicates that the greatest source of stress for an executive is from navigating change.

Help your team understand the purpose of significant changes and the importance of supporting them. Use your influence to execute on those initiatives.

## Be Respectfully Candid

With all that's been said in this chapter, it may sound like leading up means being a "yes-man" or "yes-woman." Not at all. There are times when leading up requires you to challenge your superiors. When that happens, be respectfully candid. Present your questions or concerns in a way that shows you respect your boss's position and authority.

The best leaders establish protocols for these situations. In one organization I served, we started hard conversations with the phrase, "Can I ask a clarifying question?" Another common introduction is, "Do I have permission to speak freely?" It's a respectful way to prepare your boss for a tough question or challenging discussion.

Be proactive and transparent. Don't hide important information or bad news. Chances are, that will come back to haunt you later. Instead, gather the facts and present your findings. Whenever possible, bring recommendations and solutions to the table. That's especially true if you want to challenge your boss's ideas or decisions.

Present the business case to support your suggestions or proposals. By business case, I mean a well-designed argument as to why your idea is advantageous to the organization. Many worthy ideas fall by the wayside because those who propose them don't show how the ideas will move important organizational priorities forward. Other ideas fail because they lack due diligence. Instead, show your boss that you've done your homework.

Here is a nine-part framework I suggest to my coaching clients as they make the business case for their ideas:

1. Define the problem. Most change initiatives are designed to solve problems. Create a clear and succinct description of the problem to attract attention. For example, a healthcare provider might define a patient no-show problem as, "One-sixth of our patients don't show up for their appointments due to the lack of an automated reminder system."

2. Explain the implications. Outline the consequences of the problem in the immediate term as well as long term. Help your superiors envision the repercussions of not making a change. Describe the current approach to the issue as a band-aid. As I often tell coaching clients, "Pull on the band-aid and let them feel the pain."

3. Offer potential solutions. Show that you've done your due diligence by identifying multiple solutions to the problem. Provide a summary of the alternatives you explored. Consider creating a chart that compares the critical elements of each option.

4. Present a recommendation. Offer your proposed solution and a high-level description of how it will be implemented. Explain the most significant advantages of your proposal over other options. Anticipate the question, "How much will this cost?" and outline the financial investment.

5. Identify resources. Another question that's sure to arise is, "How are we going to pay for this?" Identify potential funding sources for both up-front and ongoing costs. Determine the budget lines that will pay for your proposal or describe the financing for it. If future cost savings will fund the initiative, show the payback calculation.

6. Provide a cost-benefit analysis. Include nonfinancial costs and benefits along with the financial ones. For instance, using the healthcare example above, increased patient satisfaction and retention would be among the benefits you could present.

7. Acknowledge potential risks. Rarely are change initiatives without risk. Leaders are naturally

wary of proposals that include all benefits without acknowledging the potential for failure or setbacks. Be transparent about those risks.

8. Include criteria for measurement. This step assures your superiors that you have a long view of success. Describe how you will measure success and determine whether mid-course adjustments are necessary along the way.

9. Request a decision. A clear ask speeds the decision-making process. A lack of clarity slows it down. Prepare your request in the form of a question that compels a prompt response or at least advances the discussion.

Several months after taking a cohort of healthcare leaders through the process of making the business case, I was on a video call with the organization's CFO. "Jon, it worked," he said. "When we asked this group to submit their revised budget proposals, we could tell which leaders went through the training. They took to heart the importance of making the business case and did their homework to submit better requests. Those who followed the process and did a thorough review got approval for their proposals within ten minutes of the call."

Here's one last suggestion to be candidly respectful to your boss. When appropriate, offer to hold up the mirror for him or her, to share your experience of his or her leadership (humbly and diplomatically, of course). Ask if your boss is open to observations that could help him or her improve—focus on something specific and actionable. Helping your boss discover his or her blind spots is a gift. Everyone wins when the leader gets better. This is when building a high-trust relationship with your boss pays big dividends.

## Flip The Script: Invite Upward Leadership

As you excel at upward leadership, invite your team members to lead up to you. That might be a new concept to them, so a bit of coaching may be in order. Take the five tips I shared in this chapter about upward leadership and create talking points for a team meeting.

Guide your team members on the best ways to build trust with you. Describe what it takes for each of them to do their jobs exceptionally well. Share your preferred communication style and how they can best connect with you. Describe the best approach for team members to gain clarity about how your top priorities inform theirs. Establish ground rules for them to follow when it comes time for them to challenge you.

Don't dismiss the importance of this exercise. This chapter's opening story of the Challenger disaster is one of many pointed examples of the catastrophic failure that can occur when leaders discourage upward leadership, whether knowingly or not. The demise of former mobile phone giant Nokia provides another excellent case in point.

During the 2013 press conference announcing the sale of Nokia's cell phone business to Microsoft, CEO Stephen

Elop was reported as saying, "We didn't do anything wrong, but somehow we lost."[48] The statement was sobering, but was it true?

Just six years earlier, when Apple introduced its first iPhone, Nokia was on top of the mobile phone world. According to the technology researchers at Gartner, Nokia held a market share of nearly 38 percent—more than Motorola, Samsung, and Sony Ericsson combined.[49] As of this writing, the Nokia 1110 is still the best-selling cell phone model of all time, even outpacing Apple's iPhone 6/6 Plus.[50]

Mainstream business writers point to Nokia's lack of vision, flawed strategy, and inferior technology as causes of its downfall. A deeper analysis indicates those factors were symptoms of a more profound leadership failure. Business professors Timo O. Vuori and Quy N. Huy conducted in-depth interviews with seventy-six former Nokia top and middle managers.[51]

Vuori and Huy concluded that Nokia's culture suffered from fear. Top managers were fearful of their competitors and shareholders, while middle managers were afraid of their superiors and peers. Senior leaders intimidated middle managers with unrealistic expectations. Middle managers failed to provide their superiors with truthful information about their technical capabilities, or a lack thereof. In short, these middle managers were kept from practicing the upward leadership that could have saved the business. Nokia's fourteen-year run as the top mobile phone seller was soon over. Within a few years, Microsoft wrote off its entire

$7.6 billion purchase of the cell phone business, declaring it a failure.

## It Takes Courage To Lead Up

Leading up is an often neglected but essential function of leadership. We've seen the consequences of that neglect. Remember, you will likely spend your entire career with someone above you. The best leaders learn the delicate-yet-bold art of leading up.

Are you ready to master upward leadership? In *Leading Up: How to Lead Your Boss So You Both Win*, author Michael Useem writes, "Leading up requires great courage and determination. We might fear how our superior will respond, we might doubt our right to lead up, but we carry a responsibility to do what we can when it will make a difference."[52]

CHAPTER 4

# MISSION-CRITICAL TAKEAWAYS

1. Clarify what you need most from your boss to develop as a leader in your organization. Find ways to share those needs with your boss.

2. Evaluate your work for opportunities to gain mastery of the responsibilities and tasks that enable you to bring the most value to your organization.

3. Seek a clear understanding of your superior's top priorities and determine whether your work is structured to give them adequate attention.

4. Consider whether there is a situation that requires you to have a respectfully candid conversation with your boss. Schedule a time to meet with him or her regarding that situation.

5. Flip the script by thinking about ways you can help your team more effectively lead up to you. Be explicit about keys to a productive working relationship, communication preferences, and any hot buttons your team members should know about.

77

# CHAPTER 5

# Leading Across

W hen I was a boy, I used to admire the model rockets in the Sears catalog. They sold look-alike rockets to the ones in the Apollo program that were being sent to the Moon. In recent years, the company that published the famous catalog has fallen from grace due to an abject failure of leadership.

The company was founded by Richard Sears, who started a mail-order watch business in my home state of Minnesota, and Alvah Roebuck, who was a watch repairman. They incorporated as Sears, Roebuck and Company in 1893 and eventually became one of America's best-known retailers.

Sears held the top spot for retail sales for many decades, until Kmart surpassed them in sales in the 1980s. Sears then fell to third place in 1990 when Walmart took the lead in total sales.[53] The management of Kmart purchased Sears in 2005 and formed Sears Holdings, which continued its steady decline. In 2018, its 125th anniversary year, Sears filed for bankruptcy and is now a mere fraction of its former self.

As with Nokia, voluminous case studies will be written about the demise of Sears. They will similarly address failed acquisitions, subpar innovation, bad marketing, and other strategic errors; but they will miss the most significant root cause of all of these factors: poor leadership. In this case, CEO Edward Lampert created an ultracompetitive environment, rather than inspiring Sears's numerous brands and product lines to work together. There was no collaboration across these lines as peer-to-peer leadership was discouraged at all levels.

After taking over as CEO, Lampert restructured the company into units that were directed to compete against each other. If a division wanted to utilize IT or HR services, they were required to contract with them, with the option of contracting with entities outside of the company. The appliance division was required to pay royalties to the branding division when it sold the company's popular Kenmore appliances. That led them to feature other brands more prominently because they were more profitable. One executive told a Bloomberg investigative journalist that the situation at Sears had become "dysfunctionality at the highest level."[54]

While the lack of horizontal leadership was systemic at Sears, it's not uncommon in other organizations. Silos develop between teams and departments as their leaders fail to lead across. Once entrenched, these silos can be hard to break down and, as a result, the organization suffers. Such was the case at one client's healthcare business where conflict between the leaders of two service lines led to a decline in internal referrals between them. Instead, customers were referred to providers outside of the organization, a costly hit to the organization's revenue.

## Rely On Influence Because There Is No Role Power

Leading across is the most complex and underrated form of leadership. It is completely dependent on influence because, as you lead among peers, there is no role power between you. So the statement I previously referred to, "You're not the boss of me," can easily be used on both sides of the relationship.

Let's say you are the director of Marketing in an organization. You often need cooperation from the directors of other departments to move your objectives forward. In turn, they will need cooperation from you to move their objectives forward. Because none of you holds a "boss card" over the other, you need to rely on influence to gain that cooperation.

For example, you will need budget resources from the director of Finance to execute marketing strategy, launch advertising campaigns, and to produce marketing collateral. You also need data from Finance to measure the effectiveness of your strategies so you, in turn, can make the business case for even more resources to fund your initiatives.

At the same time, your peers in Finance need your cooperation to provide documentation to pay marketing-related expenses. That includes everything from obtaining receipts for credit card purchases to copies of contracts for more significant expenditures. Neither you nor your Finance peer can stand over the other, issuing "Because I'm the boss" demands. However, you can both develop influence that promotes a collaborative spirit between the two of you.

Three elements will help you develop greater influence among your peers, which have been aptly termed as the three Cs: Character, Competency, and Chemistry. You may have seen these elements suggested as ways to assess candidates when you're in the hiring process. Work on developing them in yourself just as much as you look for them in others.

Character has been defined by many experts as who you are when no one else is looking. Character is formed from personal integrity, which psychologist and author Henry Cloud describes as "the whole [person] working well, undivided, integrated, intact, and uncorrupted."[55] Based on Cloud's definition, we can safely add a lack of personal integrity to the list of potential leadership derailers from chapter 3. Without it, your leadership will be short-lived.

To be a person of character requires honesty—with oneself and others. Honesty encompasses more than just your words; it includes your actions and attitudes as well. Two of my favorite leadership experts are James Kouzes and Barry Posner from the Leavey School of Business at Santa Clara University. For over thirty years, Kouzes and Posner have researched the top characteristics of the most admired leaders. Their surveys gather responses from workers across six continents. Guess what characteristic came out on top—every time? Honesty.

By a long shot. Nearly 90 percent of responses include honesty as an important characteristic of admired leaders.[56]

Although honesty is essential to lead well in all directions, it's even more so in leading across. It's harder to BS your boss or direct reports than it is your peers. They may not see you in action as frequently or as closely as your boss or team members. So it may be more tempting to compromise your honesty. That choice will in turn diminish your character and, along with it, your influence. Eventually, it will cost you the opportunity to lead among your peers.

Ask one simple question to self-check your character. It comes from David Horsager, author of *The Trust Edge*. It's incredibly simple and powerful at the same time: *Am I doing the right thing?* Horsager suggests the challenge isn't in determining what's right, but making the choice to follow through and actually do it. He points to the Space Shuttle Challenger disaster as a case in point. As described in chapter 4, leadership at the O-ring manufacturer, Morton Thiokol, knew those components posed a major risk of failure in cold weather, but allowed the space shuttle to launch anyway. In this case, not doing the right thing cost seven crew members their lives.[57]

Competency is the second C-word essential to developing your influence. You need to master your craft and prove that you can do your job well. When it comes to leading your peers, they need to trust your competency and expertise in your functional area. Remember, trust is one of the precursors to influence.

Let's go back to the Marketing-Finance relationship described earlier in this section. You lose credibility if, as the Finance director, you give your Marketing colleague a budget and return later with the news your original target was thousands of dollars higher than it should have been. The Marketing team may have already committed to spending those funds, and now the team will be in the difficult position of having to revisit those commitments.

There are significant consequences for monetary failures. Other cases, like the Challenger disaster, are a matter of life or death. Fail the competency test too often and you jeopardize the influence required to lead horizontally among your peers. While no one is perfect, a loss of credibility results in a loss of influence, which will eventually cost you the ability to advance as a leader.

To build competency, create the Leadership Development Plan outlined in chapter 7. Build margin into your schedule and use downtime for self-development. Expand your network of knowledgeable professionals in your field who share ideas for growth. Find a respected mentor with a track record of peer-to-peer leadership and learn from his or her insights.

The third C-word is chemistry, which is like a glue that binds together your relationships with peers and colleagues.

Don't underestimate the importance of likeability in building these relationships.

You will find it very difficult to influence your peers if they don't want to be around you.

Start by looking for natural points of affinity with your peers. Find common ground and shared interests in the form of past work experiences, school background, and hobbies that open doors for you to get to know them. Involvement in similar community or charitable activities aid in cultivating chemistry. If you have kids, you might find their sports, music, and other activities serve as a platform for connection.

Be careful, though, to avoid the trap of sameness. Don't limit your pursuit of chemistry to colleagues with similar backgrounds and interests. Cultivate relationships with peers of diverse age, gender, ethnicity, and other demographics. Seek out those who have different points of view from your own. Building intentionally diverse relationships will expand your perspective and create a more well-rounded network. Doing so will enable you to be a more relevant leader to your organization and its external stakeholders and customers as well, which is crucial in an ever-increasingly global marketplace.

As I will share later in this chapter, developing healthy working relationships requires peers to spend time together. You will be hard-pressed to schedule time with your peers if they'd rather avoid you. Explore insights from the assessments mentioned in chapter 3 if you discover rough edges that are getting in the way of building productive relationships across the organization.

## Prioritize The Enterprise Over Your Silo

Do you want to advance to an executive level within your organization? If so, you need to learn how to think at an enterprise level, rather than being focused narrowly on your division, department or team. You may recall from chapter 3 that one potential leadership derailer is having too narrow a functional orientation. A narrow functional orientation limits your ability to see the big picture, what's best for the organization as a whole, beyond your functional area alone.

One of my healthcare clients includes this ability among their leadership competencies and describes it as having an "organization-wide mindset." It requires the ability to prioritize the success of the overall organization, acting and making decisions accordingly. It also involves a commitment to break down silos and understand the challenges faced by leaders and teams in other parts of the organization.

Those who excel at leading across create synergy, the recognition that the entire enterprise is more likely to succeed when its parts collaborate, share resources, and support one another. In turn, each of the parts will gain from that success through an increase in resources, opportunities, and recognition. Develop a reputation for driving this cycle of success and you will position yourself to lead at higher levels within your organization.

Start building this competency by identifying what leadership speaker and author Patrick Lencioni calls your "first team." Who is your first team? Lencioni puts it this way: "The team you belong to must come ahead of the team you lead: this is putting team results (i.e., organizational needs) ahead of individual agendas (i.e., the team or division you lead)."[58]

Leaders often overlook this principle and instead place their top priority on the team they lead. That's understandable. After all, the performance of your team is a direct reflection on your leadership. It's important to secure resources, build your staff, and achieve your team goals. However, when you prioritize the needs of your team over the needs of the organization, you create silos.

> Recognizing your first team will help you navigate the tensions inherent in thinking at an enterprise level.

Chances are your first team is led by your boss. The majority of the team is made up of your peers. Here are a few ways to use the first team approach to build your enterprise thinking skills:

1. Pay attention to what the leaders one level above you are focused on. That will give you an understanding of goals and priorities at higher levels within the organization.

2. Listen to the questions and issues the leaders at your level raise. That information will help you understand the challenges in other parts of the

organization, as well as opportunities for you and your team to help them.

3. Summarize your observations from these meetings and conversations for your team. This will enable your team to see the big picture and make it easier to enlist their help as you serve the greater organization.

## Build Healthy Working Relationships With Peer Leaders

Now that you understand how enterprise thinking will help you lead across to your peers and colleagues, it's time to focus on ways you can build healthy working relationships with them on an individual basis.

During the Mission-Critical Leadership Experience, I ask, "When is the best time to build a good working relationship with your peers?" Someone usually replies, "A long time ago." Although you can't turn back the clock, you can start today. You don't want to wait until you need something from one of your peers to start building that relationship.

In this section, I offer five examples for building strong working relationships from leaders I've served in my coaching practice.

Bill, the financial analyst from the story at the end of chapter 3, built a rolling schedule of coffee and lunch meetings to get better acquainted with colleagues from other departments and business lines. He viewed this approach as a way to expand his professional network within the company. Bill's initiative helped him to become better known among leaders in other parts of the organization. These meetings also enabled him to gain a better understanding of how these areas fit together, building his enterprise thinking skills.

José, a senior leader in financial services, utilized the results from assessment reports to gain an understanding of how his work style and preferences could complement or conflict with those of one of his key peer leaders. Learning about his colleague's strengths and struggles enabled José to tailor his approach to potentially difficult conversations. It also helped him anticipate when such situations were likely to arise so he could better prepare for them.

Nancy, a legal executive within a manufacturing firm, initiated a quarterly cycle of meetings with peer leaders in other functional areas of the organization. It was her approach to better understand the current challenges and priorities in each of those areas. She also found it helpful to learn of upcoming projects and contract negotiations that her team would eventually be called on to assist. Nancy compiled questions in advance of these meetings to help her show up prepared to maximize the time with her peers.

Terrell, a healthcare CFO, reached out to the new operations director in his agency while she was still in the onboarding process. He recognized the opportunity to get their working relationship off to a good start by helping her understand the organization's culture and synergies between their respective teams. Soon thereafter, Terrell gave up his room at a conference in a five-star hotel for his new peer to enjoy while he found alternative accommodations in an off-site hotel. Although he was motivated to do so out of genuine kindness, he increased his relational capital with his new peer leader.

Shawna, a VP of Finance in a technology business, reached out to colleagues soon after they were promoted to new leadership roles within their company. She viewed those promotions as a key time to affirm the productive relationships she had enjoyed with her colleagues to that point. Shawna also seized the moment to discuss important dynamics of her colleagues' new positions and how they would work together going forward.

Bill, José, Nancy, Terrell, and Shawna took a proactive approach in developing positive working relationships and gained influence with their peers. Their actions opened doors to improved communication beyond their own functional areas, enabling them to understand other parts of their organizations better. They gained important insights on the challenges and stresses their peer leaders faced, in areas like budgets, staffing, and deadlines—even pressures from their lives outside of work. They learned the best timing to approach their peers for help and discovered opportunities to offer their assistance.

Imagine: how much better would organizations run if all leaders were more intentional about building these horizontal relationships?

> A stronger focus on improving peer-to-peer relationships would reduce the organizational drag that keeps many enterprises from achieving critical goals and priorities.

Who are your most important peer relationships? How could you use the examples from Bill, José, Nancy, Terrell, and Shawna to make those working relationships more healthy and productive?

## Establish Rules Of Engagement For Working Together

Leading effectively across your organization goes beyond building stronger personal relationships with key peers. You also need to focus on how you will work together to move your organization forward. You might have a shared vision or goals with your peer leaders, but a different style or ways to accomplish them. That can lead to friction which, if not managed, will sabotage your relationship-building efforts.

I worked with two partners in a financial services business who were both highly goal-driven and results-oriented. They shared a desire to grow their business, but each one had a very different approach to determining his or her goals and mapping out a plan to achieve them. Jim was more detail-oriented and wanted a structured plan that included more specific steps, ordered in a certain sequence.

Sally preferred a more spontaneous approach, wanting to leave more flexibility to make changes over time. Being less detail-oriented, she was also less inclined to devote the time and energy to creating written plans.

As we talked, I realized that Jim and Sally faced a challenge that went beyond determining a shared vision and goals. Indeed, the challenge went beyond developing the strategy to achieve them. Their bigger challenge was to agree on how to work together in a healthy, cohesive partnership. Our discussion focused on how they could each contribute from their strengths and view their differences as complementary, not just frustrating. They made mutual commitments on how they would communicate and receive one another's ideas without judgment as they worked together.

This story illustrates the importance of creating "rules of engagement" for working together in peer-to-peer settings. When facilitating discussions about rules of engagement with workplace teams, I ask the question, "How do you play together in the sandbox?" Many organizational settings are eerily similar to my childhood experience, when the smiles and laughter of kids playing in the sandbox could so quickly turn to aggravated jostling and fighting. Have you ever experienced this type of behavior?

Rules of engagement provide a shared understanding of the communication, decision-making, resource-sharing, and conflict management standards essential for working within, and across, teams. The investment of time to develop these standards will pay dividends as teams gain an understanding of how to play the game of organizational life better. Start at the executive level and cascade the process throughout your organization, keeping in mind the "first team" concept presented earlier in this chapter.

In team coaching exercises, I ask participants to articulate these rules as commitments that each of them will espouse. To help them brainstorm ideas, I ask the team, "What mutual commitments are most essential to your working as a cohesive leadership team?" I start by suggesting one principle that seems to apply universally for all teams: Assume positive intent. Renowned leadership author John Maxwell explains the principle this way:

> *We tend to judge others according to their actions. It's very cut-and-dried. However, we judge ourselves by our intentions. Even if we do the wrong thing, if we believe our motives were good, we let ourselves off the hook. And we are often willing to do that over and over before requiring ourselves to change.*[59]

Assuming positive intent will go a long way to break down silos and promote a more collaborative environment within your organization. Adopt this mindset in your peer-to-peer relationships and help the team members you lead to develop it as well. Build the mindset into your rules of engagement.

Even after laying the important groundwork of creating rules of engagement, you will experience occasional breakdowns as you lead horizontally within your organization.

Take the fictional account of Tom and Jill, peers at an executive leadership level within a healthcare organization. Tom is the HR director. Like others in his field, he has been charged with increasing employee engagement and retention. For several months, Tom and his team worked behind closed doors on a new employee appreciation and recognition program.

Tom was excited to unveil the new program to their Executive Team. "On behalf of the HR team, I am happy to introduce a new rewards program that will increase employee engagement and retention," Tom announced. "We got the idea from rewards programs sponsored by credit card companies, airlines, and retailers. Employees earn points for demonstrating positive work behaviors. These points can be redeemed for gift cards to restaurants, stores, concerts, and sporting events."

Tom's excitement quickly turned to frustration as he encountered immediate resistance from Jill, the director of Auxiliary Services.

"Why am I hearing about this for the first time today?" she asked. "We've been working on our own program to enhance recognition and appreciation in our department."

Tom acknowledged Jill for her team's initiative but chided her for not following protocol. "Jill, I don't understand why you didn't consult with HR before moving forward on this," he retorted. "You know that anything related to employee engagement should go through HR."

"Yes, that's true," Jill replied. "But I don't understand why you kept your new program a secret for so long. You could have asked the rest of us on this team for input.

"Besides," she continued, "we decided on an approach that is more authentic and genuine. We plan to train our supervisors to offer more messages of encouragement and appreciation to their team members. We'll help them to better notice positive work behaviors that should be rewarded, but in a more personal way than giving them points."

As the discussion continued, Tom and Jill began questioning each other's intentions. Eventually, trust between the two eroded and they lost the ability to influence one another.

It doesn't have to be that way if you prepare for what one of my mentors, executive coach Donna Schilder, calls "relational accidents," a significant risk in organizational life. Communication breaks down, toes get stepped on, and people feel blind-sided. At these times, it's human nature to assume our colleagues intended to hurt us. However, that's not usually the case. That's why they're called accidents. Just like two vehicles at a slippery intersection in the middle of a Midwest winter, things start sliding out of control until they run into something else—or in this case, someone else.

The best leaders recognize that relational accidents are part of the game and know how to address them when they occur.

The key is knowing how to apologize when you cause a relational accident and how to forgive when someone collides with you.

I was surprised to find a body of research on how to offer an effective apology. Researchers at Ohio State University found one aspect of an apology to be most important: the acknowledgment of responsibility. An apology is viewed as more genuine when there's an admission of fault and acceptance of responsibility for one's action. The second most important part of an apology is the offer for repair, a willingness to fix what went wrong.[60]

Both characters in the story above have an opportunity to apologize for actions that caused the breakdown in communication. Tom could apologize for not sharing his team's plans earlier in the process, or for not seeking input from other department leaders. Jill could apologize for not consulting HR as her team started working on its own initiatives.

Apologies from Tom and Jill would be a great start, but that's not the end. They also need to learn how to forgive. In another surprising finding, I learned that there is an organization called the International Forgiveness Institute.

Dr. Robert Enright, professor of educational psychology at the University of Wisconsin, is the institute's president. He defines forgiveness as:

> *A willingness to abandon one's right to resentment, negative judgment, and indifferent behavior toward one who unjustly injured us, while fostering the undeserved qualities of compassion, generosity, and even love toward him or her.*[61]

That sounds like the opposite of most workplace environments. More often, it seems, leaders like Tom and Jill allow resentment or bitterness to set in, fracturing working relationships, creating silos, and damaging workplace culture. However, imagine if Tom and Jill replaced those negative responses with forgiveness. They could rebuild trust and strengthen their working relationship. Leading across gets easier as workers see relational accidents as inevitable, but repairable.

Whenever possible, work directly with your peer leaders to repair these accidents when they occur, and as soon as possible. There's a tendency for many people to run to their bosses to fix them; in many cases both parties share the same boss. Don't surprise your peer by going to the boss without his or her knowledge. That move will diminish the trust and influence you've been building and drive your peer conflict even deeper. Instead, lean into the challenge. Engage in difficult conversations and navigate conflict in a healthier way. Here are several tips based on my research and coaching practice:

MISSION-CRITICAL LEADERSHIP

1. Avoid triangulation, that is, talking to a third party who is not part of the problem or solution; that leads to gossip.

2. Prepare for the conversation in advance.

3. Determine your desired outcome.

4. Prioritize the relationship over being right.

5. Find common ground and points of agreement.

6. Listen with curiosity and openness.

7. Own your contribution to the situation.

8. End with agreement for moving forward.

9. Agree to not unearth prior conflicts that have been resolved.

10. Work through the process of forgiveness.

For additional study on this topic, I recommend the following excellent resources:

*Crucial Conversations: Tools for Talking When Stakes are High* by Kerry Patterson, Joseph Grenny, Ron McMillan, and Al Switzler (McGraw-Hill, 2011)

*Difficult Conversations: How to Discuss What Matters Most* by Douglas Stone, Bruce Patton, and Sheila Heen (Penguin Books, 2010)

*Fierce Conversations: Achieving Success at Work & in Life, One Conversation at a Time* by Susan Scott (Berkley, 2004)

Here is one last word on this topic—guidance for when you are the boss and have team members in conflict. There's a delicate balance between jumping in to fix the problem and taking a laissez-faire approach. I heard about one executive leader who told his team, "You're all adults, you need to figure this out," and left them to flounder on their own. The conflict had grown to a point where the coworkers could not resolve it on their own. At that point, they needed someone with role power to help them work through their difficulties and coach them through the process. Exercise wisdom to determine when to get involved and when to step back.

## Seek Win-Win Opportunities To Collaborate And Share Credit

As you become an enterprise thinker and use your influence to build positive working relationships, you will discover win-win opportunities for collaboration with peer leaders. Shawna, the finance leader mentioned earlier, worked to become proactive in seeking out such opportunities to meet with her peers. Not every meeting will yield a dramatic impact, but each one is a building block that will ultimately get Shawna noticed and enable her to advance to new levels of leadership.

I'm writing this chapter during the weekend of the SpaceX-NASA launch of astronauts Doug Hurley and Bob Behnken to the ISS. Hurley and Behnken were the first astronauts to travel in an American spacecraft since the United States space shuttle program was discontinued in 2011. They were also the first astronauts to be carried by the Falcon 9 rocket and Dragon spacecraft built by entrepreneur Elon Musk's SpaceX company, a commercial enterprise.

News media emphasized the collaborative partnership between NASA and SpaceX, a remarkable feat in and of itself. Their overarching example of collaboration is actually comprised of thousands of smaller collaborative efforts. Within both organizations, scientists, engineers, and other professionals worked together for years to make this historic event happen.

As Musk said after the launch, "It is the culmination of an incredible amount of work by the SpaceX team, by NASA and by a number of other partners in the process of making this happen. You can look at this as the results of a hundred thousand people roughly when you add up all the suppliers and everyone working incredibly hard to make this day happen."[62]

At two key points in their journey, Hurley and Behnken recognized the widespread, collaborative effort that led to their moment in history. In doing so, they offered another important lesson for leaders: to share credit generously with peers and colleagues for their contribution.

The first of these points occurred once the Dragon vehicle separated from the Falcon 9 rocket, propelling the astronauts toward the ISS. After a congratulatory message from the Falcon 9 launch team, the astronauts replied:

> *Congratulations to you and the F9 team for the first human ride for Falcon 9 and it was incredible. Appreciate all the hard work and thanks for the great ride to space. Proud of you guys and the rest of the team. Thank you so much for what you have done for us today, putting America back into low-earth orbit from the Florida coast.*[63]

The second point occurred after the Dragon successfully docked with the ISS. Once again, Hurley and Behnken shared their accomplishment with the greater team:

> *It's been a real honor to be just a small part of this nine-year endeavor since the last time a United States spaceship has docked with the International Space Station. We have to congratulate the men and women of SpaceX at Hawthorne, McGregor, and at Kennedy Space Center. Their incredible efforts over the last several years to make this possible cannot go overstated. We'd also like to thank Kathy Leaders and her team of the Commercial Crew Program of NASA. An outstanding job by everyone. We'd also like to thank the men and women of the National Aeronautics and Space Agency. This is an incredible time to be at NASA.... We thank you again and congratulate you.*[64]

After being congratulated by ground crews from NASA and SpaceX, the astronauts again emphasized the team effort behind their accomplishment:

> *We appreciate all the good words and everyone thanking us, but it truly was a magnificent effort by the entire team. The SpaceX team, the NASA team, and the team across America who was able to pull this off and bring human space flight again to our nation. Thanks for everything.*[65]

Being generous in sharing credit with your collaborative partners will breed a greater cooperative spirit among your peers. This generosity creates a positive cycle that leads to more opportunities for successful collaboration in the future. As you excel in leading across with your peers, your superiors will take notice and open the doors for advancement within the organization.

# MISSION-CRITICAL TAKEAWAYS

1. Assess your ability to influence others by evaluating yourself against the three Cs: character, competency, and chemistry. Determine how you can strengthen each of these areas.

2. Reflect on recent decisions and discussions to determine whether you prioritize the higher-level needs of your organization over those of your own department or team.

3. Change your mindset regarding the "first team" you serve and develop an organization-wide mindset.

4. Identify one peer leader with whom you can develop a stronger relationship and schedule a meeting to discuss opportunities to collaborate on organizational priorities.

5. Review recent work accomplished by you and your team on cross-functional initiatives and find wins for which you can generously share credit with others outside of your team.

# CHAPTER 6

# Leading Down

O n Thursday, July 17, 1975, a scrawny thirteen-
year-old boy loaded about thirty newspapers into
a yellow bag with padded shoulder straps. He
walked through the neighborhood, placing them at the doors
of subscribers to the old *Minneapolis Star*, the once-popular
afternoon newspaper in Minnesota's largest city.

The headline that day celebrated the docking of the United
States Apollo spacecraft with its counterpart from the Soviet
Union, the Soyuz. Three astronauts and two cosmonauts
shook hands and began their scientific experiments at the
center of the joint mission.

Officially known as the Apollo-Soyuz Test Project
(ASTP), this mission was widely hailed as a symbol of
détente, or the attempt to ease strained relations, between
the two countries. In many ways, ASTP set the tone for
cooperation that eventually led to the ISS.

That reality was lost on the newspaper carrier, though. I know that for a fact, because I was the one delivering the evening news. My mission was simply to get my deliveries done on time, hopefully resulting in generous tips from my customers.

Although I didn't realize the significance at the time, it was also my first chance to experience leadership in a workplace environment. My boss was the regional delivery manager, Mr. Charland. He proudly wore a large Navy class ring that signified his military background. He also drove a brown sports car that reminded me of the Pontiac Firebird driven by James Garner in *The Rockford Files* television show.

Mr. Charland served as an early role model of leadership for me. On one hand, he set high expectations for prompt delivery and respectful interactions with customers. On the other, he realized we were kids and was quick to extend grace and encouragement when needed.

Mr. Charland understood the importance of the two Rs of leadership—results and relationships—in his interactions with us. Those dimensions are crucial to Mission-Critical Leadership, especially when leading those over whom you have authority in your organization.

## The Traditional View Of Leadership

As stated earlier, most leadership development is focused on a singular direction: downstream on the organizational chart. It's about leading the people for whom you are "the boss"—your direct reports and other subordinates. So, it follows that most leadership books would start with this chapter. But here we are in chapter 6. What makes Mission-Critical Leadership unique is the recognition that the best leaders lead well in all directions, not just downward.

## Build Your Leadership Style On Trust And Influence

Chapter 4 explored the importance of mastering upward leadership by building trust with your superiors. Chapter 5 covered how crucial influence is when leading across, peer-to-peer, within your organization. Trust and influence are essential to leading down as well.

Relying on role power to lead your direct reports is short-sighted—a rookie mistake, if you will. Eventually, your team members will resent your "because I'm the boss" approach and stop responding to it. On the other hand, as you continue to establish trust and influence with them, you will build a team ready to follow your lead to accomplish the vision and goals in front of them.

During the Mission-Critical Leadership Experience, I ask participants, "How can you earn trust and influence with your team members?" Initial responses usually mention the importance of character, such as acting with integrity or being trustworthy. Many participants highlight the importance of the leader's know-how and expertise to help get the team's work done. Others emphasize the need for leaders to care about their workers as people, to be genuinely interested in their well-being.

In other words, it takes proficiency in both of the two Rs of leadership to win the trust and influence necessary to lead your team well.

> You must demonstrate that you can achieve results *and* build relationships.

Results are crucial to show your workers that they are playing on a winning team; no one wants to play for a loser. They need to see that you're making meaningful progress toward important goals. At the same time, your workers want to know they're not being used as a means to an end, but that you have their best interests in mind.

From my own experience, I was most engaged in my work when serving under such leaders. They are the leaders for whom I would readily run through a brick wall if the situation called for it. Even years later, I would show up if one of those leaders called me to join them in a cause, or to fight a battle.

One of the best ways to infuse your leadership style with trust and influence is to develop a "coach approach." Early-career workers desire to work for bosses with a coaching style, rather than one based heavily on role power. Brain science research affirms the effectiveness of coaching as a leadership practice.[66]

One reason coaching is so powerful is that it focuses on the whole person, not just the problem. Professional coach training emphasizes the importance of coaching the "who," not just the "what." Coaching is a collaborative approach that empowers workers to take greater ownership for their own growth and development. It enables them to gain skills and experiences that will serve them in future roles, not just the one they're in now.

I focus on five essential skills when training leaders to develop a coach approach. These skills are part of the competency model espoused by the International Coach Federation, a credentialing body for professional coaches.[67] The following is a summary of these skills.

**Active listening**. The United States Institute of Peace defines active listening as "a way of listening and responding to another person that improves mutual understanding."[68] Active listening involves talking less—professional coach training suggests the coach talk no more than twenty percent of the time. The best listeners focus fully on and observe the other person, avoiding distractions that take their attention away. They read nonverbal communication and offer subtle cues that they are tracking with the other person. In coaching, active listening also involves listening for what's not being said and being alert for what that communicates.

**Powerful questions**. By asking perceptive questions, you reflect listening and understanding to the other person. Questions help you clarify meaning, encourage discovery, and generate insights. They are also effective in challenging assumptions without being argumentative. Use powerful questions to help your team members move closer toward their goals. For example, if they are stuck on an important project, a simple question such as, "What is your next step?" will help them formulate a plan to move forward.

**Delivering feedback.** Like coaching, early-career workers crave frequent and immediate feedback. It's part of the world they've grown up in. Most video games are built on constant feedback that helps frame your next move. Think about the last time you stayed at a hotel. You likely received a survey asking for feedback on your stay. One entrepreneur. com article offers five steps to productive feedback:

1. Create safety.
2. Be positive.
3. Be specific.
4. Be immediate.
5. Be tough, not mean.[69]

**Goal setting and action planning.** Coaching is forward looking, helping the people being coached to reach their potential. Use coaching to help your team members create specific goals that enable them to move forward toward that potential. Before wrapping up your coaching conversations, ensure your team members are clear on those goals and the action steps to meet them. The SMART acronym is an effective tool: set goals that are specific, measurable, attainable, relevant, and time-bound.

**Supportive accountability**. Use accountability to promote your coachees' learning and development. Follow up on their commitments from prior coaching conversations. Affirm their progress and challenge them positively when needed. Encourage self-discipline so they are not dependent on you to ensure they carry out their commitments. Healthy accountability involves supporting coachees without letting them off the hook.

## Embody The Organization

As a leader, one of your key responsibilities is to uphold the mission, vision, values, and strategies of your organization, including policies and procedures. Visualize yourself as the conduit, carrying these elements from higher levels of the organization. You are responsible to uphold them and to convey them to your team. You also need to set a good example by modeling behaviors consistent with them.

Many leaders get caught in the quagmire, stuck in the middle between their organization and team members. It's easy to succumb to complaints from team members about an unpopular directive, or even to let your own disapproval leak out in how you present such directives to your team. That's not fair to your team, because it forces them to choose between following the organization or following you as their superior.

Eventually, that dilemma encourages subtle—or not-so-subtle—rebellion on your team. The dilemma also creates organizational drag, which prevents the organization from moving forward on important goals and initiatives. Trust me, there are enough forces already preventing progress from being made.

Consider it an opportunity to practice leading up anytime you find yourself in disagreement with organizational directives. See chapter 4 for more specific guidance on upward leadership. If disagreement occurs too often, ask whether you are still a good fit with your employer. Constant disagreement is a sign that you're working in the wrong place and would be better served by working in an organization whose mission, vision, and values you can more fully support.

## Communicate With Clarity And Consistency

If you were to narrow the myriad of skills to the one set that will make or break a leader, communication would be at the top of my list. Effective communication is essential to Mission-Critical Leadership. I doubt you are surprised by that fact. When I ask leaders about the top challenges in their organization, communication typically lands among the top three issues.

What makes good communication so difficult? We have more tools than ever before, yet rarely do I find leaders who claim they've solved their communication challenges. In fact, it's usually the opposite. Having more tools seems to make communication even more challenging.

Developing strong communication skills starts with understanding the basics. In his book, *Organizational Communication*, Alan Zaremba establishes five criteria for effective communication:

**Timely.** The person you are communicating with receives your message when the information is meaningful. No one wants to be invited to a meeting just before it starts, or worse, after it has already taken place.

**Clear.** Your message conveys the intended information and is understandable to the person who receives it. Continuing with the meeting example, your invitation makes it clear whether attendance is required or optional.

**Accurate.** The information in your message is factually correct, i.e., details for the date, time, and place of the meeting are well-defined and true.

**Pertinent.** Your message is relevant to the person receiving it. Group emails risk violating this principle as the message may not pertain to all recipients. The problem is compounded when the email chain continues with "reply all" responses.

**Credible.** Your reputation as the sender is trustworthy and dependable. Recipients can believe your message and rely on it as they determine an appropriate response.[70]

All five criteria work together to make communication effective. When one is lacking, gaps occur and communication breaks down. For example, your meeting invitation may be accurate in stating that it will be held at half past seven in the conference room. If there is more than one conference room, however, recipients may go to the wrong one. Or, if your organization operates beyond the typical business day, there could be confusion as to whether the meeting is at half past seven a.m. or p.m. Your message lacks the specificity required for clarity.

Communication expert Skip Weisman identifies the lack of specificity as the first of "the 7 Deadliest Sins of Leadership & Workplace Communication." Weisman states that nonspecific information leaves out important details or uses words with the potential for multiple meanings that lead to misunderstanding.[71] In most cases, I would characterize the lack of specificity as falling into lazy communication habits. In others, it may be an insidious way to set people up to fail. Either way, leaving specific information out of your communications diminishes the trust required for successful leadership.

> Whenever you experience a communication breakdown within your team, go back to these fundamentals.

Ask your team members which of these criteria was flawed. Determine how they can become more aware of the deficiency and work together to overcome it in future communications.

## Use The Best Communication Tool Available

Another common weakness in organizational communication is failing to use the most appropriate tool for communicating. Email or another form of digital communication is often the guilty culprit. The proliferation of email over the past twenty-plus years may have contributed to more communication miscues than anything else.

I recall an incident dating back to when email first became common. One of my team members, Maria, approached me, visibly upset by an email message she received from a peer in another department. Her colleague responded to a seemingly innocuous question by questioning Maria's integrity. It was a hard blow to Maria's conscientious nature. As we discussed the situation, it was clear that her colleague could have chosen a more appropriate vehicle to respond to Maria's question.

Zaremba uses the term "media richness" to describe the best form of communication for the circumstances. Media richness reflects the communication medium's capacity to change the understanding of a message between two or more parties. It is dependent on opportunities for immediate feedback, the presence of verbal and nonverbal communication cues, and the capacity to tailor the message to personal circumstances (versus communicating to a larger group). In general, the more instantaneous interaction a communication tool provides, the better.

During communication training workshops, I break participants into small groups and hand them a stack of ten cards representing a variety of communication tools. They range from highly interactive forms such as face-to-face meetings and video conferences to less interactive forms like email, personalized memos, and bulk mail. For fun, I throw in a card for Morse code. Each group sorts the cards in order of media richness and presents the reasons for their ranking.

This exercise leads to a productive discussion of common communication pitfalls. I raise questions such as:

"What is the best vehicle to communicate a significant error or oversight with one of your customers?"

"How would you address a performance issue with one of your direct reports?"

"What is the best way to communicate with your supervisor when you want to request a day off on short notice?"

These questions prompt a deeper awareness of opportunities to improve communication.

I'm often asked what it takes for leaders to improve communication within their teams. It starts with a mindset of continuous improvement, always honing their communication skills. As Paul, a successful entrepreneur and business owner, stated in my interview with him, "We are never satisfied. I think we work harder at this than most businesses, but we're constantly trying to get better. Sometimes it's an addiction."

## Get To Know Your People

No one wants to be treated as a cog in a wheel. Yet, that's often how employees feel. They feel valued only for what they produce. Beyond that, they crave to be known as real people, who have their own goals and dreams. They want their leaders to recognize their career interests and talents and help them fulfill their individual potential, as well as to make a more meaningful contribution to the organization.

As a leader, it's crucial for you to get to know your team members at a deeper level. This is another opportunity to lean into the relationships side of leadership. Start by learning about who they are outside of work. By doing so, you demonstrate an interest in them as a person, beyond as a worker. Ask questions like: Where did you grow up? What did you want to be when you grew up? Tell me about your family. What do you most enjoy doing outside of work? What are you looking forward to this weekend?

Then, gain a better understanding of your team members' work style, preferences, strengths, and struggles. Utilize assessment tools such as those discussed in chapter 3 to gain deeper insights about each team member. Leverage these insights to create a positive work environment that enables them to thrive and grow. Use the reports to prepare professional development plans for each individual.

Sharpen your power of observation to identify hidden strengths your team members aren't aware of. Show them their potential career growth and encourage them to pursue opportunities to advance. We had a catchy acronym for this at a church where I served as a volunteer leader: ICNU. Say it out loud: "I see in you." Reflect on leaders across your lifetime who saw potential in you and encouraged you to pursue goals and achievements you would not have dreamed possible on your own. Do the same for your team members.

In *Talent Magnet: How to Attract and Keep the Best People*, Mark Miller suggests that one key to retaining top talent is to help them realize a brighter future.[72] Collaborate with your team members to discover a compelling vision for their career. Help them chart a course that will eventually make that vision a reality. Provide opportunities for them to gain the experience and learn the skills for the next step along the way.

Beware of tendencies to hold onto people in ways that stunt their professional growth. Instead, master the skills of equipping and empowering. Use your coaching skills to encourage their self-development as a supplement to the development you provide.

Learn what motivates your team members. Traditional forms of motivation, such as incentives and bonuses, have a limited shelf life. Susan Fowler, author of two stellar books on motivation, describes such methods as creating suboptimal motivation, which is short-lived. Optimal motivation, on the other hand, is aligned with one's values, integrated with how someone sees himself or herself. Such motivation is inherent, coming from within the person rather than from external sources. Fowler suggests that the essence of motivation is related to three critical psychological needs: choice, connection, and competence.[73] When these needs are met, people thrive and flourish, because an innate desire that is present in all of us is satisfied.

Choice refers to the need for autonomy, the sense of having some control or choice about what someone does, or how it's done. This doesn't mean leaders are hands-off, or laissez-faire, but that they allow their employees to have input about the work they perform.

Connection relates to a sense of belonging to others, as well as a sense of purpose. People desire to be part of something bigger than themselves and to enjoy working with others in the process. Miller challenges leaders to offer a bigger vision in response to their team members' desire to make a difference.[74] Herein lies a powerful opportunity for you, as a leader, to help people find meaning in their work and be part of a healthy team environment.

Competence represents the need for growth and learning over time. It's about feeling qualified and equipped to handle the normal, everyday challenges of the job. Leaders play an important role here as well since the workplace is where people spend the most time. Not feeling competent in the workplace can negatively impact other parts of workers' lives as well.

## Recognize Effort, Appreciate Performance, And Celebrate Achievement

We are currently experiencing a significant appreciation deficit in the workplace. Based on a 2019 study by TINYpulse, an employee engagement solution provider, about three-quarters of workers feel undervalued at work.[75] Gallup's research indicates only one in three workers received praise or recognition for their work in the preceding week.[76] The appreciation deficit is very costly: 66 percent of workers say they are likely to leave their current jobs due to a lack of appreciation.[77] In the meantime, these workers become more disengaged, diminishing their performance on the job.

> Most leaders have good intentions about showing appreciation to their team members. Those intentions fall by the wayside as their day-to-day work drowns them in a myriad of other details.

Or, they're like Matthew, whose drive for results propelled him forward so fast that he neglected to pause long enough to celebrate his team's achievements. As I interviewed his team members, several mentioned that he was off to the next goal or project before they could enjoy what the team had just accomplished.

Brian, a healthcare CEO, recognized this tendency within his organization. As we planned for the Mission-Critical Experience, he shared results from a recent employee engagement survey. The survey revealed that while employees expressed a willingness to go the extra mile to serve their customers, they didn't feel appreciated for making that effort.

Brian recognized that eventually, the failure of their leaders to appreciate their team members would erode the staff's discretionary effort.

As we got to this topic during their leadership gathering, Brian presented his concerns. Rather than prescribing a magic formula to get his leadership team to show more appreciation, I posed the question, "As you look at your colleagues around the room, who stands out as an example of a leader who does this well?"

Almost immediately, one member of the team pointed to one of her peers and said, "Julie does a great job of showing appreciation. She notices when her team members do a good job and stops to thank them. She writes a lot of thank you notes, not just for her team but people in other departments, too." Other leaders nodded in agreement with the selection of Julie as an example.

Julie sat straighter and taller in her chair as she listened to her colleagues' praise. She seemed a little embarrassed to be singled out as I approached her. "You've been named as a role model for showing appreciation in this organization," I said. "What's your secret sauce?" I asked. "How do you do this so well?"

Not surprisingly, Julie offered a humble and self-deprecating response. "I've never thought about what I do as being that special," she answered. "I guess it comes naturally for me." When I pressed Julie to dig deeper on why her colleagues singled her out as an example, she said, "I'm careful to notice when someone is working hard or does a good job. And I try to say thank you or send them a note right away, so I don't forget."

Julie's comment led to a conversation about the leader's power of observation, or what leadership expert Ken Blanchard describes as catching your team members doing something right. In his book, *The New One Minute Manager*, he emphasizes the importance of giving "one minute praisings" at those times.[78]

What if giving praise and recognition doesn't come as naturally to you as it does for Julie? Find ways to build a habit of recognition into your routines. Steve, a healthcare CFO, does a walk-through of his department near the end of each business day, thanking each member of his team for his or her work. As he described his daily practice, he realized that his trip through the office could become rote. To make his expressions of thanks more effective, Steve decided to share something more specific he had observed. For example, he could say to a team member, "Thank you for noticing the error on the invoice you reviewed today. I appreciate that you caught the error and contacted the vendor without being asked."

Mandy, a manufacturing executive, was interested in Steve's example but admitted she was likely to forget in the midst of all of the other demands on her time. When I asked what would prompt her to remember, she replied, "Well, I suppose I could put a reminder on my phone." Mandy's tone indicated she wasn't sold on her own idea. When I probed further, she said, "The idea of setting up a reminder on my

calendar seems very elementary. I shouldn't have to do that."
Yes, a phone reminder may seem elementary; but it's often
as simple as that to establish important habits that will make
you a better leader.

## Conduct Regular One-on-One Check-in Meetings

The one-on-one check-in meeting is the meta-strategy
for leadership. It's the one approach that will help you
encompass all of the practices discussed in this chapter.
From personal experience, these check-ins have been a game
changer. I often reflect on seasons during my career when
I was at my best leadership, in comparison to when my
leadership was at its worst. The biggest difference between
those seasons? I consistently held one-on-one check-in
meetings with my team members during the best seasons
and neglected them during the worst seasons. If only the
difference had been more obvious at the time!

What makes the one-on-one check-in so powerful? It's
a perfect opportunity to build influence through coaching,
communicating well, getting to know your people, and
recognizing their work, together in one conversation or a
series of regular conversations.

If the one-on-one check-in is so powerful, why is it so
easy to overlook? In my coaching work, I've discovered four
primary reasons why leaders neglect these critical meetings.
Number one is their reluctance to add another meeting to
the calendar, because they think it takes too much time.

Number two is the constancy of deadlines, which prioritizes the work getting done over discussions about how it can best be done. Number three is the span of responsibility many leaders carry—the more direct reports a leader has, the more likely he or she will ignore one-on-one meetings. Number four is a lack of structure to optimize the one-on-one conversation and keep it from drifting to an unfocused chat that is eventually seen as a waste of time.

Here is a framework to help you overcome those obstacles and maximize your one-on-one check-in meetings:

**Determine who to include**. Generally, you will want to connect one-on-one with every one of your direct reports. There may also be someone at a level below your direct reports whom you include in your check-in meetings, i.e., an emerging leader you are mentoring or someone in line for a promotion that will make him or her a direct report in the near future.

Determining who to include is more complicated in professional service firms and matrix forms of organizational structure, where workers may have more than one direct supervisor. In these cases, you should match supervisors and subordinates based on the primary supervisory relationship. Alternately, you can look for natural affinity that increases the likelihood of check-in meetings happening. The bottom line is to ensure every employee in the organization has a regular one-on-one conversation with someone in leadership above them.

Think about other directions on the organizational chart, too. If you're not already having regular one-on-ones with your boss, request that you put them on the calendar moving forward. These meetings provide a platform for upward leadership. If you have key relationships outside of your team, consider adding them into your check-in cycle as a way to build your skills in leading horizontally.

**Schedule check-ins at regular intervals**. Coordinating your calendar with the individuals you want to meet with regularly may be the most challenging aspect of scheduling one-on-ones. Remember, if the one-on-one check-in is your X-factor to become a better leader, such meetings should be elevated among your scheduling priorities. These meetings don't need to be very long. Once you develop the routine, a twenty- to thirty-minute check-in should suffice for most of your direct reports. The increase in remote work makes Zoom and other video-based platforms a viable meeting "place" when it's not possible to meet in person.

Two primary factors will drive the frequency of check-ins: the number of your direct reports and the amount of time and experience each of them has in their roles. As your team of direct reports gets larger, the longer the interval between check-ins. You need to meet more frequently with employees who are new to the team or to their roles. A team member assigned to a complex project needs more regular attention, as do team members whose roles are experiencing significant change.

**Keep a running list of agenda items**. I trained my team members to keep a "Jon List" to track the questions, concerns, and ideas for our next check-in meeting. I kept a similar list of the items I wanted to bring to their attention. This is one way that one-on-ones can save you time in the long run. It keeps your team members from coming to you with one-off issues that can wait—they know they will have opportunity to discuss them in the next check-in.

**Start with your team member's agenda**. Let your team members present the items on their agendas first. That gives you an opportunity to gauge whether they recognize what should be their top priorities as well as other issues of concern. It also provides an opportunity to observe anything that may be weighing them down. Over time, I found that my direct reports covered most of the items on my agenda.

**Add your points**. Once your team member completes his or her list, present any items from your list that have not been covered. Beyond the tactical discussion, use this time to check more deeply on the team member's experience in your workplace and under your leadership. Add comments that inspire your team member's professional growth and development. If you find that your entire time is consumed by tactical discussion, schedule a separate check-in for developmental conversations.

**Close with clear follow-up actions**. Each check-in meeting should end with clear follow-up steps, both for your team member and for you as a leader. These steps should include a plan for reporting on follow-up actions after they are completed, whether in the next check-in meeting or at some point in between.

One-on-one check-in meetings are a perfect avenue to practice the coaching techniques presented earlier in this chapter. You may be tempted to turn this meeting into a monologue, during which you tell your team member what to do and what not to do. After all, you are accustomed to being the expert and solving problems.

That's the trap that Brenda, a nonprofit manager, fell into. Although she called her check-ins coaching sessions, she did most of the talking and left her team members feeling like they couldn't get a word in edgewise. Resist that temptation. Take the advice of one of my coaching mentors and bite your tongue if you tend to talk too much. Leverage the long-term value of the check-in to develop and retain your best team members. That won't happen if they aren't engaged in the conversation.

## Leading Down In A Whole New World: Remote Leadership

If remote work is part of your workplace reality, strive to sharpen five specific tools that will help you lead better in a virtual environment: empathy, mutual expectations, coaching skills, elevated communication, and team development.

## Empathy

A slow return to their "normal" offices means many workers will continue to face dynamics that made the shift to remote work incredibly challenging. Some are sharing the work-from-home environment with a family member or roommate who is also working from home. In the early stages of the pandemic, schools closed, classes moved online, and parents took on more responsibility for their kids' education. Many parents are concerned that they will continue to shoulder that increased level of responsibility. Adding to their weight are limitations on other options for their kids—childcare options, youth sports, music lessons, and recreational activities that have been cut back or closed altogether.

Leaders must show empathy toward workers who face these challenges. Daniel Goleman, a thought leader on emotional intelligence, refers to empathy as the ability to understand the emotional makeup of others and make intelligent decisions with those emotions in mind.[79] That compels leaders to focus on their employees' emotional well-being and go beyond merely asking, "How are you?" Practice active listening and observation to read between the lines as you talk with team members about their situations and, when it's appropriate, to invite a deeper discussion of their needs.

## Mutual Expectations

Demonstrating empathy toward your employees will make you aware of the need for an individualized approach in setting expectations with them. Notice my choice of the word *with* rather than the word *of.* Establishing mutual expectations requires a collaborative effort rather than issuing across-the-board mandates. The work-from-home dynamics mentioned above will vary dramatically from one employee to the next.

Work style and personality differences also affect how each team member responds to working remotely versus in a traditional setting. Some people crave the more structured environment of an office, while others welcome the flexibility and freedom of working away from it. Also, the jobs performed by your team members may differ significantly in their suitability for remote work. For some jobs, there's little difference in how they are performed remotely. For others, there are significant barriers. Acknowledging and navigating these differences will build trust with your team members.

As you collaborate with workers to establish mutual expectations, consider these three critical factors. First, how much flexibility they have in setting work hours and whether they need to be available during certain core hours. Second, expectations about their accessibility for meetings, phone calls, emails, and other communication, internally and externally. Third, deadlines for projects or important milestones and whether they are recurring or one-time events.

## Coaching Skills

Performance and productivity coaching was gaining traction as a leadership tool before the pandemic, especially among early-career workers. It is even more important now as leaders are forced to rely less on fixed performance demands and instead must collaborate with workers on mutual expectations, as discussed above. Coaching is effective in helping workers not only understand *what* work needs to be done but *how* to get it done productively—especially since staying productive can be challenging for employees not accustomed to working remotely or being in a more chaotic home environment.

Research during the pandemic revealed a wide disparity in workers' assessments of their productivity while working remotely. In a YouGov study sponsored by *USA Today* and LinkedIn, 54 percent of respondents indicated that working from home had a positive impact on productivity. In comparison, 25 percent said it hurt their productivity.[80]

Through coaching, leaders can help team members identify barriers to productivity and explore ways to overcome them. One CFO coached a struggling employee to reorganize her desk at home to replicate her setup at the office, complete with three monitors (which the company purchased for her). Another finance leader used regular check-in calls to identify and mitigate common distractions that were interfering with her team's ability to focus well enough to complete essential tasks.

## Elevated Communication

Increasing communication is essential anytime there is significant change or crisis. A shift to remote work makes this even more true. The need for more communication starts at the top, as leaders convey the organization's vision and top priorities during the current environment. In my role as an adjunct faculty member for North Park University, I was faithfully reminded by the university president throughout the pandemic of two crucial priorities: the health and safety of the community and the successful completion of the academic term.

Conduct regular one-on-one check-in meetings with remote team members. These check-ins may be shorter in duration than if you were working together in person. The increased frequency helps to substitute for subtle communications that we take for granted in the office, such as informal conversations at the coffee pot, along the cubicle wall, or in the hallway that provide an opportunity for quick updates, questions, and clarifications. Those in-person interactions that allow leaders to read body language and nonverbal cues to gain a sense of how their team members are doing are lost in a remote environment. Although not a perfect solution, regular video check-ins are a helpful way to replicate such interactions in a virtual environment.

One executive offers a special Zoom meeting room during specific dates and times for this purpose. Another schedules virtual office hours for drop-in conversations with team members. Do not be an absentee boss, even with top performers who work well on their own.

## Team Development

According to the YouGov survey cited above, more than half of employees feel lonely as a result of remote work, with about 20 percent saying they are lonely all or most of the time.[81] You can combat the isolation factor by hosting virtual team gatherings. Encourage collaboration within the team to move critical projects forward. There is an increased willingness within many teams to share the workload and ensure critical tasks get done.

When possible, add a social element to your team building with nonwork events like a virtual happy hour, scavenger hunt, or trivia contest. If your online events are growing stale, invite your team to brainstorm new ideas. When done well, these gatherings build trust and positive relationships within the team.

Team development is even more challenging in a hybrid environment, where some employees work in an organization's office and others work remotely. In these cases, protect your team members from feeling like second-class citizens, especially if they are in the minority based on their work location.

Consider pairing in-office and out-of-office workers to ensure each group stays connected with their counterparts. Creating a buddy system is also helpful to enhance the feeling of connectedness for new employees who work remotely, when they haven't worked in an in-person setting among peers, where they can learn your organization's culture.

Put these five leadership tools to work and the result will be a healthier, more collaborative, and more productive team.

# MISSION-CRITICAL TAKEAWAYS

1. Review your working relationship with each of your team members. Look for any relationships where trust has been frayed or broken and determine your next step to repair those relationships.

2. Adopt a coach approach to your interactions with team members. Select one team member with whom you intentionally practice the coaching skills described in this chapter.

3. Evaluate your communication style and practices. Determine your most frequent communication breakdowns and identify habit changes that will close those gaps.

4. Visualize each of your team members and select one person who needs you to show appreciation. Be specific in the action or performance that you identified.

5. If you aren't already conducting regular one-on-one check-ins with your direct reports, begin scheduling them. If you are already doing one-on-ones, ask each team member to suggest one potential change that would make them more effective.

# PART III

# SUSTAINING AND MULTIPLYING YOUR LEADERSHIP

# CHAPTER 7

# Take Your Leadership To The Next Level

I t's up to you. What's next? How will you take your leadership to the next level?

Continuous improvement is at the heart of Mission-Critical Leadership. As Craig Groeschel, the lead pastor of one of the largest churches in the world, says, "When a leader gets better, the entire organization gets better."[82]

Take your leadership to the next level by answering three critical questions:

- How are you doing now?

- What will it take for you to get better?

- How will you make it happen?

## How Are You Doing Now?

Before you can get better, you need a clear evaluation of how you are doing as a leader today. There are two parts to this evaluation: self-reflection and feedback from others.

## Self-Reflection

Leaders are often left gasping for air as they get swept up in the whirlwind of today's fast-paced, ever-changing marketplace. It's hard for them to slow down and reflect on their leadership. But you must learn to press the pause button if you are serious about mastering Mission-Critical Leadership.

Schedule an appointment with yourself, away from your office, to reflect on your leadership journey. Retrace your steps, starting with your earliest leadership experiences. Review your successes and failures at each stop along the way, noting important lessons that shaped you as a leader.

Make meetings like this a regular habit to evaluate your performance as a leader.

> Create a mental movie of recent leadership moments and how you showed up in them.

Explore what went well and how you made a positive impact. Identify what didn't go well and how you contributed to the breakdown. Determine the changes you need to make in your approach to leadership to make it more effective.

Assessments offer guided self-reflection that unearth new discoveries about your leadership. I administer the Path4/Path6 instruments from RightPath Resources for many of my clients. They gain valuable insights on how their strengths and struggles shape their leadership effectiveness in each direction.

## Feedback From Others

Self-reflection is a good start, but it will leave you with a one-sided view of your leadership if you stop there. The second step to determine how you're doing is to obtain feedback from the people you lead. Getting feedback is like asking someone to hold up a mirror for you, so that you can see how others experience your leadership.

Conducting a 360-degree feedback assessment is a great way to get input from others. Earlier, I referred to the composite 360 that sparked an interest that eventually led to this book. These surveys are typically completed anonymously online, with your work relationship being the only identifier (i.e., boss, peer, or direct report). Most of these instruments include a self-assessment which can be used to compare how you rate yourself with the ratings of others.

The anonymous nature of this feedback is both a blessing and a curse. The blessing is the ability for your colleagues to share their experience without fear of judgment or reprisal.

That's the curse, too. Without clear direction, the 360 survey can be used as a tool for retaliation or other punitive motivation. The administrator of the survey, typically an HR professional or external coach, should emphasize that it is for developmental, not disciplinary, purposes.

Another downside to the typical 360 assessment is its cost. For that reason, many organizations limit this tool to senior leaders. Don't let that stop you from seeking feedback on your own. I call it the DIY (do-it-yourself) 360.

In a popular *Harvard Business Review* article, Kristi Hedges suggests the following approach:

- Select five colleagues (I suggest your boss, two peers, and two direct reports).

- Arrange face-to-face meetings (which could be done via Zoom in a remote work setting).

- Stay open and resist the urge to become defensive (take a deep breath and remind yourself that this conversation will help make you a better leader).

- Ask two simple questions:

  1. What's the general impression of me in the workplace?

  2. What could I do differently that would have the greatest impact on my success?[83]

To obtain specific feedback in a certain area, consider modifying the second question. For example, if you sense a need to improve the way you lead meetings, you might ask,

"What could I do differently to make the meetings I lead more successful?"

You don't need to wait for a structured 360 exercise to obtain feedback. You can use the two questions above at any time, with any person who is willing to share from their experiences with your leadership.

## What Will It Take For You To Keep Improving?

After gathering feedback, it is time to create a structured plan to improve and grow as a leader.

Build your Leadership Development Plan (LDP) on the following four components:

**Leverage your strengths.** What are your top strengths? How do they show up when you are at your best as a leader? How can you leverage them to improve your team and the organization you serve?

**Develop your skills.** What skills do you need to develop to be a better leader in your current role? What skills do you need to prepare for the next level of leadership? How can you practice those skills now?

**Mitigate your struggles.** What are your biggest struggles as a leader? How do they detract from your effectiveness as a leader? What can you do to prevent these tendencies from hurting your leadership?

**Employ your resources.** What resources will be most helpful to your leadership development? Who are the best people to enlist to help you along the way? What books, publications, podcasts, and training programs provide the knowledge and inspiration to help you grow?

## What's Your Plan?

The most successful participants in my leadership programs treat their plans as living, breathing documents and update them regularly. They use their LDPs as tools for regular discussion with colleagues who are committed to their growth and development as leaders.

Half of the participants in one program were promoted to the next leadership level in their firms within a matter of months. Tanya, a technology consultant, told me that she still refers to her plan from time to time two years later.

Marshall Goldsmith, regarded as the world's best executive coach, works with leaders to engage key stakeholders in an ongoing process of feedback and follow-up. He recommends that, once you obtain feedback, you share your intentions for improvement with these stakeholders. Then, follow up with them regularly to measure progress in each growth area.

Goldsmith suggests asking questions like, "Based on my behavior last month, what ideas do you have for me next month?" Focusing on future behavior, rather than dwelling on the past, inspires continued improvement. Goldsmith's advice is worth following—he built his stakeholder-centered coaching methodology on the premise that he is only paid if his clients achieve positive change in their leadership behaviors.[84]

## How Will You Make It Happen?

Count Microsoft founder Bill Gates among those who agree with Goldsmith regarding the importance of feedback.

"Everyone needs a coach," said Gates at the beginning of his 2013 TED talk. "It doesn't matter whether you're a basketball player, a tennis player, a gymnast or a bridge player." The audience laughed as his slides first showed world-class athletes and then a picture of Gates himself sitting at a card table.

"We all need people who will give us feedback," Gates continued. "That's how we improve."[85]

Take it from Bill Gates. If you want to take your leadership to the next level, get coaching.

The International Coach Federation defines coaching as "partnering with clients in a thought-provoking and creative process that inspires them to maximize their personal and professional potential."[86]

I define coaching as helping people follow through on their good intentions, even if that means helping to discover what those intentions are.

Your coach can be someone within your organization; many larger companies offer internal coaching arrangements. Senior leaders with a passion to develop emerging leaders often make good coaches. Your boss might be a good candidate to serve as your coach; but if you're not careful, your coaching conversations will be more tactical than developmental.

Select a coach who is deeply committed to your growth as a leader and who is willing to ask tough questions. Choose someone who understands that the essence of coaching stems from dialogue rather than telling his or her worn-out stories. It is an engaging process of discovery and exploration to help you find your way as a leader, rather than trying to copy another leader's approach.

> Whenever possible, enlist help from an external coach as well.

Again, some organizations provide outside coaches at certain levels of leadership. If not, invest your own time and resources in coaching. Rhonda, a CFO in the construction business, approached me after a leadership presentation at an industry conference. She wanted outside help to walk through several leadership challenges in her organization.

Leaders often ask whether I work with a coach myself. "Yes, I eat my own cooking," is my typical response. Rick Erisman has been my coach for several years. His coaching helps me clarify my top goals and create actionable steps to achieve them. Rick has an uncanny ability to help me identify and break through the barriers and obstacles to my success—most of which, incidentally, show up every time I look in the proverbial mirror. I often describe that insight as the greatest value from coaching: discovering and overcoming the ways I interfere in my own progress. If it wasn't for my coaching with Rick, this book might never have been written!

## Your First And Best Coach

Ultimately, it's not your coach who is most responsible for your development as a leader. It's you.

Occasionally, I hear complaints from leaders who lack development opportunities in their organizations. "I don't feel like I'm being developed," they say.

My response is always, "Don't wait for someone else to develop you. Don't rely on your boss or your company. Develop yourself."

Never in history have there been such plentiful resources for self-development as a leader. As I write this chapter, a Google search on the word "leadership" returned over 2.6 billion results. A search on Amazon provided over 60,000 resources on leadership.

Read books from renowned leadership thinkers like Whitney Johnson, Tony Dungy, and Charlene Li, as well as the writers quoted in this book. If you don't like to read, listen to the audiobooks. You can also listen to podcasts featuring these same experts and others. Forbes.com and other business websites regularly publish lists of the best leadership podcasts. Dave Stachowiak's *Coaching for Leaders* podcast is an outstanding all-purpose leadership podcast.

Attend leadership conferences, such as the Global Leadership Summit held every August. Many conferences shifted to a virtual format, in part or in whole, during the COVID-19 pandemic. Online options for leadership training and development are almost unlimited. The LinkedIn

Learning platform alone provided over 3,600 resources as of this writing.

Developers are now using artificial intelligence to create individualized resources for leadership development. Rocky is an application billed as "The Leadership Coach in Your Pocket," with daily coaching and self-reflection questions, along with curated content on essential leadership skills. The basic version is an excellent supplement to person-to-person coaching at a reasonable price.[87]

Coach Amanda was introduced by LeadX as an "HR Chatbox Executive Coach." Text your leadership challenges and questions to Amanda and she will respond with tips on topics like giving feedback and delegation. The application integrates with a personality assessment that enables Amanda to personalize advice to your needs. It also includes behavioral nudges to remind you to follow through on the leadership actions and habits you're trying to develop.[88]

## Never Stop Learning

Leaders are learners. However you decide to go about it, never stop learning. Continuous learning is essential to adapting your leadership due to ever-increasing changes in the marketplace.

Business author Chip Bell illustrates this truth by sharing the story of Masaru Ibuka, who founded the company that later became Sony. Early on, Ibuka recognized the importance of learning to stay competitive in the electronics industry. Rather than focusing on learning new technologies alone, he worked to develop the ability to learn within his organization.

In one interview, Ibuka explained, "We knew learning was a skill. The more employees learned, the better learners they became. We knew continuous learning would make them more adaptive to new ways of manufacturing." This intense focus on continuous learning led Sony to become one of the most successful and highly-respected electronics companies in the world.[89]

NASA Astronaut Scott Kelly, who served on three voyages to the ISS, suggests that leaders model the willingness to take risks, trying things that haven't been done before, and engaging in continuous learning throughout the process.[90]

What can you do to keep an intense focus on continuous learning?

# MISSION-CRITICAL TAKEAWAYS

1. Take the do-it-yourself 360-degree feedback challenge and find opportunities to improve your leadership from it.

---

2. Find a coach, mentor, or accountability partner to help you develop your LDP and implement it.

---

3. Identify your go-to sources for continuous learning and create a regular process to access their content. Find at least one new source for learning that will stretch you outside of your comfort zone.

---

# CHAPTER 8

---

# The Next Frontier: Your Leadership Impact

Elon Musk may be eccentric, but he's certainly not boring. When his seventh child was born in May of 2020, Musk and his partner, the singer Grimes, gave their son a name that included characters not recognized in the English language, which they shortened to X.

Musk accumulated significant wealth in the early 2000s as a large investor in PayPal, which was purchased by eBay. During that same era, Musk founded SpaceX and took over control of automaker Tesla. In an unusual partnership between the two companies, Musk launched a Tesla vehicle into space on a SpaceX rocket, complete with a mannequin in the driver's seat.

Musk has a wide variety of other interests: launching satellites to provide wireless internet service across the world, boring long-distance tunnels for electric vehicles, developing an air-cushioned system for high-speed travel, and sponsoring research to integrate the human brain with artificial intelligence. You see, he hates traffic jams and is concerned that, if not corralled, artificial intelligence will endanger the human race.

Under Musk's leadership, SpaceX ushered in a new era of space travel with its Falcon 9 rocket. The Falcon 9 delivered astronauts Doug Hurley and Bob Behnken to the ISS during the summer of 2020. Much to Musk's relief, SpaceX returned them safely to Earth after over two months in space. Musk told the two astronauts' families he felt personally responsible for their well-being.[91]

In his celebratory remarks, Musk expressed a sigh of relief. He made it clear that while Hurley and Behnken's mission was a great feat, it was only one step toward a much bigger goal, to land people on Mars. Ultimately, Musk wants to establish a human colony on Mars and live there himself.

Musk's passions fuel his tireless pursuits of the next frontier. His endeavors to make a difference in the world are endless. The same can be true of your leadership.

Your next frontier is all about impact, the difference your leadership will make in the lives of others.

In this final chapter, I provide a framework for you to design the next frontier of your leadership, including the difference you want it to make.

## Your Leadership Impact Statement

An old television commercial for frozen pizza posed the question, "What do you want on your TOMBSTONE?" The brand name is capitalized because, in a clever twist on words, that was the name of the pizza company.

It's a classic question, useful in provoking you to think about your legacy. That's true of life as well as leadership. However, legacy is often a back-to-the-future way of thinking, focusing on how you will be remembered after you leave this earth—that is, if you're not heading on Elon Musk's journey to Mars.

What if, instead of legacy, you thought more about impact? What impact do you want your leadership to have on the people you lead? This question provokes thinking about what you can do now to elevate your impact as a leader, and it will also help you focus on the next frontier. You have a choice. You can create the next frontier and establish your leadership impact by design.

Your Leadership Impact Statement will encompass the following sections:

- Your leadership journey
- Your leadership point of view
- Your leadership style

- Your leadership impact

In each section, you will find questions to guide you in compiling the stories, ideas, and information you need for this exercise. Start with simple bullet points in response to each question. At the end, I will explain how to pull everything together into a powerful Leadership Impact Statement.

Don't stop reading now! I promise, this will be the most significant and long-lasting value you gain from this book.

## Your Leadership Journey

- How would you describe your leadership journey?
- What experiences have most shaped your leadership?
- How have other leaders influenced your ideas about leadership?

The first section of your Leadership Impact Statement requires a trip down memory lane. Retrace your steps to the earliest leadership experiences you remember. I encourage coaching clients and workshop participants to return to their childhood, recalling leadership in school sports or their first jobs. Others go back to memories as the firstborn child in their family, or leadership experiences among kids in their neighborhood.

Reflect on how those experiences shaped your leadership. Some of them will generate positive memories when your leadership was effective or made a difference.

Other experiences may be painful, such as times when your leadership either failed or didn't turn out according to plan. Note the lessons learned from those experiences, even if you weren't cognizant of them at the time. In many ways, hindsight is indeed twenty-twenty.

In addition, reflect on the people whose leadership you experienced throughout your journey. Again, this question may take you back to childhood, as you think about teachers, coaches, and youth leaders. Which leaders did you respect and want to emulate? What insights did you gain about what it means to be a good leader? Which leaders were examples of what not to do as a leader? How do those insights show up in the way you lead today, for better or worse?

## Your Leadership Point Of View

- What is your definition of leadership?
- What do you view as the essentials of leadership?

During the 1980s, Noel Tichy was the head of General Electric's Leadership Center, serving under legendary CEO Jack Welch. In his book, *The Leadership Engine*, Tichy emphasizes the importance of leaders developing other leaders, not just followers. In fact, he goes so far as to suggest that you're not a true leader if you don't develop other leaders.[92]

To develop leaders, Tichy suggests you need to first determine your leadership point of view. In its simplest form, your leadership point of view captures your big ideas about leadership. Once you establish your leadership point of view, you determine how you will communicate it to others. Over time, it becomes inextricably linked with your practice and teaching of leadership. It serves as one of the footings in the foundation for your leadership impact.

In chapter 2, I offered definitions of leadership from experts like John Maxwell and Henry Cloud. I also offered my definition of Mission-Critical Leadership:

> Using influence to build relationships and deliver results in all directions within an organization, accelerating it faster and further toward its mission.

Now, it's your turn. It's crucial to establish your own definition of leadership. How do you define leadership?

Review the thoughts gathered in Your Leadership Journey to inform your responses to these questions. Also, draw on what you have learned in this book and other resources. Remember, this is your definition, so feel free to create it to fit your context or your expression of leadership.

Narrow these insights down to a succinct, memorable statement. You may not be able to distill leadership down to a single word, as Maxwell did, but don't make it complicated. You will use this definition as a basis for discussions about leadership throughout your next frontier.

Next, identify your big ideas about leadership, or the essentials of what makes someone a great leader. For example, in his book, *Good to Great*, Jim Collins describes the Level 5 leader as "an individual who blends extreme personal humility with intense professional will." [93]

You have learned two of my big ideas about leadership by reading this book. One idea involves the two Rs of leadership; the need to succeed in delivering results as well as building relationships as you lead. The second is the Mission-Critical Leadership framework; the best leaders lead well in all directions, not just down the organizational hierarchy to their direct reports and team members.

## Your Leadership Style

- How would you describe your leadership style?
- What would be most helpful for others to know about what it's like to experience your leadership?

I recall an instance, early in my career, when I was interviewing a candidate for a job opening at my firm. Near the end of the interview, I asked the candidate if he had any questions for me. "How would you describe your leadership style?" he asked. I'm embarrassed to admit now that I wasn't prepared for that one. I don't recall my response but I'm sure it wasn't very helpful.

> The question did force me, though, to think more carefully about how I led and what it was like to work under my leadership.

The concept of leadership style is not a new one. Back in the 1930s, psychologist Kurt Lewin introduced three basic leadership styles which are described below, using a simple decision-making scenario as an example:

- An autocratic or authoritarian leadership style: The leader makes the decision without obtaining input from others.

- A democratic or participative leadership style: The leader makes the decision after obtaining input from others.

- A laissez-faire or delegating leadership style: The leader allows others to make the decision.[94]

Your predominant leadership style probably leans toward one of these styles, while incorporating elements of all three. Remember, the best leaders adapt their leadership style to the situation at hand. They recognize that leadership is a role to play. Like Tom Hanks in his best film roles, they match their approach to what is needed from their leadership in the moment.

In the 1990s, Paul Hersey and Ken Blanchard created what is now called the Situational Leadership II model. The leader employs a combination of directive and supportive behaviors to match the developmental needs of the follower. As the competence, commitment, and confidence of the follower increases, the leader's style shifts from a directing, to a coaching, then to a supporting, and finally to a delegating style.[95]

Use your basic understanding of these leadership styles to describe your own style. In addition, incorporate such descriptors as "visionary," "inspiring," "collaborative," "get-it-done," "strategic," "results-oriented," and others, to capture the essence of the way you lead.

As you craft your own description, ask people who serve under your leadership how they would describe your style. Go back to the five individuals you consulted during your do-it-yourself 360 assessment from chapter 7. You can also reconnect with others who have experienced your leadership in a variety of situations.

Incorporate their insights with those from your self-reflection into a three- to four-paragraph summary that explains your approach to leadership. Include your primary strengths along with your biggest struggles to provide an accurate picture of your leadership style. This section of your Leadership Impact Statement will enable you to articulate what others can expect from you as a leader.

## Your Leadership Impact

- What impact do you desire to have as a leader?

- What difference will your leadership make in the lives of those you lead?

- What can you do to make your desired impact a reality?

- Who are you developing as a leader?

There is no question that your leadership will have an impact on the people you lead. The question is what kind of difference you will make. Use the last section of your Leadership Impact Statement to describe the impact you desire and how you will make it happen.

Refer to the work you did on your personal foundation in chapter 3 as you prepare this section. Your vision, purpose, and mission statements will inform the impact you hope to make as a leader in the future. It is the next frontier of your leadership.

My next frontier is best described in my mission statement:

> *I work with organizations to develop leaders everyone wants to follow, to build teams no one wants to leave, and to deliver exceptional results.*

My impact statement takes the mission a step further, getting more specific about the leaders, teams, and results where I want to make a difference. It also answers the "How?"

question, incorporating a strategy to leverage the Mission-Critical Leadership framework for greater impact.

Don't settle for less when declaring the magnitude of difference you want to make. Aim high and be aspirational as you describe your desired impact. For example, John Ramstead, one of my mentors and the author of *On Purpose with Purpose: Discovering How to Live Your Best Life*, aims to help one million leaders each achieve their desired impact. With his coaching, speaking, writing, and podcasts, John is well on his way to achieving his goal.

As an example, here are excerpts from Leadership Impact Statements written by participants in recent leadership programs:

"I hope that my leadership pushes the individuals and groups I lead to set high expectations for themselves and others."

"I want to cultivate individual talents and get people in the right spots. I want to foster a culture of responsible and respectful team members. I want them to know they are capable and that they have me in their corner to rely on."

"I want my team to know and remember that I care about their professional development and care about them as people."

"The impact I want to have is showing that leadership doesn't have to look the same as it always has. A leader doesn't have to be CEO of an organization. All of us can lead no matter the level we are at. I want to empower younger leaders to lead early and often."

Finally, identify and engage with other leaders or aspiring leaders you want to develop. Remember Tichy's point: you aren't a true leader unless you're developing other leaders.

## Write Your Leadership Impact Statement

Now you are ready to write a one- to two-page essay that covers each of the four sections for your Leadership Impact Statement: your leadership journey, point of view, style, and impact. Use your bullet points to create a more structured outline. After you list your main points, write three to four paragraphs for each section. Be thorough enough to capture the essence of each section, while being concise enough to use your completed statement as a tool to develop and encourage other leaders.

Once you complete your Leadership Impact Statement, begin presenting it to others, at least in a summarized fashion. Focus extensively on your Leadership Point of View, as that section contains your most significant beliefs about leadership and what it takes to be successful as a leader. Use the last section of your statement, Your Leadership Impact, to identify the leaders and aspiring leaders you want to reach and develop.

Don't limit your outreach to individuals who are behind you in their leadership journey. Your Leadership Impact Statement is a powerful tool to help you lead well in *all* directions.

Engage your boss and other superiors in a theme of continuous improvement. Exemplify the mantra, "When the leader gets better, everyone gets better," by encouraging their growth as leaders. Support their development by sharing helpful books, articles, and podcasts on leadership.

Join like-minded peers and colleagues in an ongoing conversation about leadership. When appropriate, share real-life challenges and partner as peer coaches to improve as leaders. Find ways to collaborate on building a culture of leadership throughout your organization.

Find emerging leaders to teach, coach, and mentor. Share your leadership journey and point of view with them. Invite them to shadow you so they can observe your leadership in action. Be open about your successes and failures, along with the lessons learned from them.

As you develop other leaders, you multiply your impact, extending it well beyond what you can do on your own. That is the ultimate payoff from leading well in all directions.

# MISSION-CRITICAL TAKEAWAYS

**1.** Retrace the steps of your leadership journey, identifying key milestones, influential leaders, and the lessons you learned along the way.

**2.** Identify people, places, and opportunities where you can make a bigger impact as a leader.

**3.** Write your Leadership Impact Statement and share it with your coach, mentor, or accountability partner. Then, begin sharing it with emerging leaders you want to invest in.

# Acknowledgments

Writing this book has been one of the most exhilarating, frustrating, strange, and rewarding experiences of my professional life (that may be worth a separate book). As I reflect on this unique experience, I'm thankful for several people whose support, encouragement, and expertise made it possible:

My Lord Jesus, "for the gifts and the calling of God are irrevocable" (Romans 11:29, English Standard Version). Only through His grace do I have the relationships and experiences that make these leadership insights possible.

My family, as they navigated the twists and turns of a jagged career path with me. I'm grateful for my wife, Barb, whose penchant for risk-taking and adventure eclipses mine, stretching me beyond my comfort zone for nearly forty years.

My kids and their spouses, Rob (Jessica), Kendra (Nate), and TJ (Sonja), who we enjoy immensely. I'm sure at times they thought their dad was off his rocker. I can't forget the precious littles, June, Leighton, Reagan, Griffin, and perhaps more grandchildren to come, whose future inspires me to press forward on my mission to develop better leaders and organizations.

My parents, Bob and Jan Lokhorst, whose love and encouragement is endless.

Faculty from my Master's program at Regent University who affirmed my writing skills and planted the first seeds of ideas for this book: Dr. Stone, Dr. Doublestein, Dr. Wiater, and Dr. Gomez in particular.

My friend and mentor, John Ramstead, for inviting me into several experiences that launched my passion for leadership into a viable business.

A more recent friend and mentor, Mark LeBlanc, a legend in the professional speaking business, whose challenge on September 4, 2019 moved this book from an idea on the back burner to a real goal with a sense of urgency.

Rick Erisman, my personal coach, for keeping the vision for this project in front of me and helping me persevere through the added noise and distraction of the COVID-19 pandemic.

Henry DeVries, Denise Montgomery, and the team at Indie Books, for guiding me through the process, being patient when progress stalled, cleaning up my shortcomings, and adding their indispensable expertise to make this book a reality.

Dozens of coaching, training, and speaking clients who provide an outlet to share these insights with the marketplace and put them to the test in real-life leadership situations.

Finally, the remarkable bosses, colleagues, and team

members I had the privilege of serving alongside at Wallace, Lokhorst & Company, YouthWorks, Hume Ministries, Covenant Pines, and Covenant Harbor. Also, the staff and fellow volunteers in churches that provided a wealth of leadership opportunities over the years. Our shared experiences laid the groundwork for much of what I understand about leadership. There are far too many of you to list, but you know who you are.

# About The Author

Jon Lokhorst, CPA, PCC, is a leadership coach, speaker, and author. He is the founder of Lokhorst Consulting LLC.

Jon works predominantly with finance and healthcare organizations to develop leaders everyone wants to follow, build teams no one wants to leave, and deliver exceptional results.

As a result of his work, organizations increase employee engagement, reduce turnover, break down silos, and build flourishing leadership pipelines that produce future leaders from within.

Jon started his professional career as a Certified Public Accountant (CPA) with an eighteen-year career at a firm that later became Wallace, Lokhorst & Company, Ltd., where he served as managing partner. He then spent fifteen years in the not-for-profit sector serving primarily as a chief financial officer (CFO) and development director.

Jon earned his undergraduate degree from Bethel University (St. Paul, Minnesota) and his Masters in

Organizational Leadership from Regent University (Virginia Beach, Virginia). He is recognized as an Professional Certified Coach (PCC) by the International Coach Federation.

Jon serves as adjunct faculty in the School of Business and Nonprofit Management at North Park University (Chicago). A member of the National Speakers Association, Jon serves on the Board of Directors of the Minnesota Chapter.

On a personal note, Jon loves grandparenting and being "Papa" to his four adorable littles, as he calls them. He's also an avid and long-suffering fan of Minnesota's professional sports teams, cheering on the Twins, Vikings, and Wild.

Learn more about Jon Lokhorst at his LinkedIn page: www.linkedin.com/in/jonlokhorst/ or by visiting his company's website at www.lokhorstconsulting.com. Contact him regarding coaching and speaking engagements via email at jon@lokhorstconsulting.com or by phone at 612-381-6275.

# Endnotes

1    Mary Baker, "Gartner HR Survey Reveals 41% of Employees Likely to Work Remotely at Least Some of the Time Post Coronavirus Pandemic," April 14, 2020, https://www.gartner.com/en/newsroom/press-releases/2020-04-14-gartner-hr-survey-reveals-41—of-employees-likely-to-.

2    Esther Shein, "PwC CFO survey: More layoffs anticipated and more people will work remotely permanently," *Tech Republic*, April 27, 2020, https://www.techrepublic.com/article/pwc-cfo-survey-more-layoffs-anticipated-and-more-people-will-work-remotely-permanently/.

3    Jessica Snouwaert, "54% of Adults Want to Work Remotely Most of the Time After the Pandemic, According to a New Study from IBM," *Business Insider*, May 5, 2020, https://www.businessinsider.com/54-percent-adults-want-mainly-work-remote-after-pandemic-study-2020-5.

4    Amanda Prahl, "Biography of Dorothy Vaughan, Groundbreaking NASA Mathematician." ThoughtCo., accessed June 22, 2020, https://www.thoughtco.com/dorothy-vaughan-4686791.

5    Margot Lee Shetterly, "Dorothy Vaughan Biographys," NASA, accessed June 22, 2020, https://www.nasa.gov/content/dorothy-vaughan-biography.

6    "Dorothy Vaughan (nee Johnson)," NASA, accessed June 22, 2020, https://crgis.ndc.nasa.gov/crgis/images/2/29/VaughanBio.pdf.

7    Carol Patton, "What's Keeping HR Up at Night in 2020?" *Human Resource Executive*, February 17, 2020, https://hrexecutive.com/whats-keeping-hr-up-at-night-in-2020/.

8    "Who First Originated the Term VUCA (Volatility, Uncertainty, Complexity and Ambiguity)?" U.S. Army Heritage and Education Center, retrieved June 15, 2020, http://usawc.libanswers.com/faq/84869.

9    John C. Maxwell, *The 21 Irrefutable Laws of Leadership: Follow Them and People Will Follow You* (Nashville: Thomas Nelson, 1998).

10  "What is Leadership? An Interview with Dr. Henry Cloud," October 4, 2016, Dr. Henry Cloud's Leadership University [audio podcast], retrieved from https://leadershipuniversity.libsyn.com/hclu-001-what-is-leadership-an-interview-with-dr-henry-cloud?utm_source=feedburner&utm_medium=feed&utm_campaign=Feed%3A+LeadershipUniversityPodcast+%28The+Leader%27s+Panel%29.

11  Dr. Henry Cloud, *Boundaries for Leaders: Results, Relationships, and Being Ridiculously in Charge* (New York: HarperCollins Publishers, 2013).

12  Jim Harter, "4 Factors Driving Record-High Employee Engagement in U.S.," Gallup, February 4, 2020, https://www.gallup.com/workplace/284180/factors-driving-record-high-employee-engagement.aspx.

13  Harter.

14  Karen Mishra, Lois Boynton, and Aneil Mishra, "Driving Employee Engagement: The Expanded Role of Internal Communications," *International Journal of Business Communication* 51, No. 2 (2014): 183-202, doi:10.1177/2329488414525399.

15  Randall J. Beck and Jim Harter, "Why Great Managers Are So Rare," Gallup, accessed June 22, 2020, https://www.gallup.com/workplace/231593/why-great-managers-rare.aspx.

16  "Why Your Employees Hate Teamwork," *Business News Daily*, March 24, 2020, https://www.businessnewsdaily.com/9616-employees-hate-teamwork.html.

17  "Chart Book: The Legacy of the Great Recession," Center on Budget and Policy Priorities. June 6, 2019. https://www.cbpp.org/research/economy/chart-book-the-legacy-of-the-great-recession.

18  "2020 Census Will Help Policymakers Prepare for the Incoming Wave of Aging Boomers," United States Census Bureau. December 10, 2019. https://www.census.gov/library/stories/2019/12/by-2030-all-baby-boomers-will-be-age-65-or-older.html.

19  William Harwood, "Fixing Hubble's blurry vision," *Spaceflight Now*, April 23, 2015, https://spaceflightnow.com/2015/04/23/fixing-hubbles-blurry-vision/.

20  Leo Widrich, "Why We Have Our Best Ideas in the Shower: The Science of Creativity," *Buffer* (blog), September 7, 2018, https://buffer.com/resources/shower-thoughts-science-of-creativity/.

21 Rohan Pearce, "What went wrong with the Hubble Space Telescope (and what managers can learn from it), CIO, March 29, 2012, https://d2r9nfiii89r0l.cloudfront.net/article/420036/ what_went_wrong_hubble_space_telescope_what_managers_can_ learn_from_it_/?.

22 John C. Maxwell, *The 21 Indispensable Qualities of a Leader* (Nashville: Thomas Nelson, Inc., 1999).

23 Scott Berinato, "That Discomfort You're Feeling Is Grief," *Harvard Business Review*, March 23, 2020, https://hbr.org/2020/03/that-discomfort-youre-feeling-is-grief.

24 Miriam Kramer, "Italian Astronaut Recounts Near-Drowning in Spacesuit (Video)," *Space.com*, August 27, 2013.

25 John Ng, "What is Self-Leadership?" *Leadership.Com.SG* (blog), accessed May 11, 2020, http://www.leadership.com.sg/person/self-leadership/what-is-self-leadership/ - .XrmNhKhKgdU.

26 Charles C. Manz, "Taking the Leadership High Road: Smooth Surface or Potholes Ahead?" *Academy of Management Perspectives* 29 No. 1 (2015): 132-151.

27 Dayana S. Sejeli and Nurnaha A. Mansor, "Leadership Derailment: Does Self-Leadership Matter?" *International Journal of Economics and Financial Issues* (2015): 522-526.

28 Paul Toscano, "Portfolio's Worst American CEOs of All Time," last modified January 29, 2014, https://www.cnbc.com/2009/04/30/ Portfolios-Worst-American-CEOs-of-All-Time.html.

29 Christian Plumb and Dan Wilchins, "Lehman CEO Fuld's Hubris Contributed to Meltdown," last modified September 14, 2008. https://www.reuters.com/article/uk-lehman-backstory-idUKN1341059120080915.

30 Travis Kalanick, "A Profound Apology," last modified March 1, 2017, https://www.uber.com/newsroom/a-profound-apology.

31 Michele Gorman. "Yogi Berra's Most Memorable Sayings." *Newsweek*, September 23, 2015. https://www.newsweek.com/most-memorable-yogi-isms-375661.

32 Michael Z. Hackman and Craig E. Johnson, *Leadership: A Communication Perspective* (Long Grove, Ill.: Waveland Press, 2013).

33 Hackman and Johnson.

34 *May 25, 1961: JFK's Moon Shot Speech to Congress.* May 25, 2011. www.space.com/11772-president-kennedy-historic-speech-moon-space.html.

35 Christopher P. Neck, Charles C. Manz, and Jeffrey D. Houghton, *Self-Leadership: The Definitive Guide to Personal Excellence* (Thousand Oaks, Cal.: SAGE Publications, 2016).

36 Stephanie Vozza. "Personal Mission Statements of 5 Famous CEOs (And Why You Should Write One Too)." *Fast Company.* February 25, 2014. https://www.fastcompany.com/3026791/personal-mission-statements-of-5-famous-ceos-and-why-should-write-one-too.

37 Andrew Bryant and Ana L. Kazan, *Self-Leadership: How to Become a More Successful, Efficient, and Effective Leader from the Inside Out* (New York: McGraw-Hill, 2012).

38 Tom Rath, *StrengthsFinder 2.0* (New York: Gallup Press, 2007).

39 Jerry W. Mabe, *Develop You, Develop Your Team...on the RightPath* (CreateSpace Independent Publishing Platform, 2012).

40 Robert B. Kaiser and Darren V. Overfield, "Strengths, Strengths Overused, and Lopsided Leadership," *Consulting Psychology Journal: Practice and Research* 63 (No. 2, 2011): 89-109.

41 Christopher P. Neck, Charles C. Manz, and Jeffery D. Houghton, *Self-Leadership: The Definitive Guide to Personal Excellence* (Thousand Oaks, CA: SAGE Publications, 2016).

42 Andrew Bryant and Ana L. Kazan, *Self-Leadership: How to Become a More Successful, Efficient, and Effective Leader from the Inside Out* (New York: McGraw-Hill, 2012).

43 "Three Black Female Astronauts Share Their Small Steps, Giant Leaps," NBC News, April 16, 2016, https://www.nbcnews.com/news/nbcblk/three-black-female-astronauts-share-their-small-steps-giant-leaps-n546641.

44 Howard Berkes, "30 Years After Explosion, Challenger Engineer Still Blames Himself," *MPR News,* January 28, 2016, https://www.npr.org/sections/thetwo-way/2016/01/28/464744781/30-years-after-disaster-challenger-engineer-still-blames-himself.

45 Berkes.

46  Sarah Kaplan, "Finally Free from Guilt over Challenger Disaster, Engineer Bob Ebeling Dies in Peace," *Chicago Tribune*, March 22, 2016, https://www.chicagotribune.com/os-robert-ebeling-challenger-engineer-dies-in-peace-20160322-story.html.

47  Clay Scroggins, *How to Lead When You're Not in Charge: Leveraging Influence When You Lack Authority* (Grand Rapids, MI: Zondervan, 2017).

48  Iulia-Cristina Uta, "Why Did Nokia Fail?" *Brand Minds* (blog). July 10, 2013. https://brandminds.ro/why-did-nokia-fail/.

49  "Gartner Says Worldwide Mobile Phone Sales Increased 16 Per Cent in 2007," February 27, 2008, https://web.archive.org/web/20130613083120/http://www.gartner/com/newsroom/id/612207.

50  "The 20 Best-Selling Phones of All Time." *Technobezz* (blog). January 27, 2020. www.technobezz.com/best/the-20-best-selling-phones-of-all-time/.

51  Timo O. Vuori and Quy N. Huy, "Distributed Attention and Shared Emotions in the Innovation Process: How Nokia Lost the Smartphone Battle." *Administrative Science Quarterly* 61, no. 1 (March 2016): 9-51. doi:10.1177/0001839215606951.

52  Michael Useem, *Leading up: How to Lead Your Boss So You Both Win* (New York: Three Rivers Press, 2001).

53  Stanley Ziemba, "Sears Slips to No. 3 in the Retail Kingdom, Behind Wal-Mart, K," *Chicago Tribune*, February 21, 1991, https://www.chicagotribune.com/news/ct-xpm-1991-02-21-9101170011-story.html.

54  Michal Rozworski and Leigh Phillips, "Failing to Plan: How Ayn Rand Destroyed Sears," *Verso* (blog), July 18, 2019, https://www.versobooks.com/blogs/4385-failing-to-plan-how-ayn-rand-destroyed-sears.

55  Dr. Henry Cloud, *Integrity* (New York: HarperCollins Publishers, 2006).

56  James Kouzes and Barry Posner, *The Leadership Challenge: How to Make Extraordinary Things Happen in Organizations* (San Francisco: The Leadership Challenge, 2012).

57  David Horsager, *The Trust Edge*, (Minneapolis: Summerside Press, 2009).

58   Patrick Lencioni, *The Advantage: Why Organizational Health Trumps Everything Else in Business* (San Francisco, Jossey-Bass, 2012).

59   John C. Maxwell, *Leadership Gold: Lessons I've Learned from a Lifetime of Leading* (Nashville: Thomas Nelson, 2008).

60   Roy J. Lewicki, Beth Polin, and Robert B. Lount, Jr., "An Exploration of Effective Apologies," *Negotiation and Conflict Management Research* 9, no. 2 (2016), 177-196, https://doi.org/10.1111/ncmr.12073.

61   "Enright Forgiveness Inventory," Mind Garden, accessed June 3, 2020, https://www.mindgarden.com/95-enright-forgiveness-inventory.

62   Sean Potter, Ed., "NASA Astronauts Launch from America in Historic Test Flight of SpaceX Crew Dragon." Last modified June 4, 2020. https://www.nasa.gov/press-release/nasa-astronauts-launch-from-america-in-historic-test-flight-of-spacex-crew-dragon.

63   "Making History: NASA and SpaceX Launch Astronauts to Space?" NASA, May 30, 2020, video, https://www.youtube.com/watch?v=pMsvr55cTZ0.

64   "NASA Astronauts Arrive at the International Space Station on SpaceX Spacecraft," NASA, May 31, 2020, video, https://www.youtube.com/watch?v=pyNl87mXOkc.

65   "NASA Astronauts Arrive at the International Space Station on SpaceX Spacecraft."

66   David Rock, *Quiet Leadership: Six Steps to Transforming Performance at Work* (New York: HarperCollins Publishers, 2006).

67   "Core Competencies," accessed May 16, 2020, https://coachfederation.org/core-competencies.

68   "What is Active Listening?" United States Institute of Peace, accessed May 18, 2020, https://www.usip.org/public-education/educators/what-active-listening.

69   Scott Halford, "5 Steps for Giving Productive Feedback," *Entrepreneur*, accessed May 13, 2020, https://www.entrepreneur.com/article/219437.

70   Alan Zaremba, *Organizational Communication* (New York: Oxford University Press, Inc., 2010).

71  Skip Weisman, *The 7 Deadliest Sins of Leadership & Workplace Communication 2.0* (Poughkeepsie, NY: Weisman Success Resources, 2012), http://wcesitefiles.s3.amazonaws.com/pdf/whitepapers/pdfs_7deadliestsinsofleadershipcomm.pdf.

72  Mark Miller, *Talent Magnet: How to Attract and Keep the Best People* (Oakland, CA: Berrett-Koehler Publishers, Inc., 2018).

73  Susan Fowler, *Master Your Motivation: Three Scientific Truths for Achieving Your Goals* (Oakland, CA: Berrett-Koehler Publishers, Inc., 2019).

74  Mark Miller, *Talent Magnet: How to Attract and Keep the Best People* (Oakland, CA: Berrett-Koehler Publishers, Inc., 2018).

75  "The 2019 Employee Engagement Report," TINYpulse, accessed May 16, 2020, https://www.tinypulse.com/hubfs/EE%20 Report%202019.pdf.

76  Annamarie Mann and Nate Dvorak, "Employee Recognition: Low Cost, High Impact," last modified June 28, 2016, https://www. gallup.com/workplace/236441/employee-recognition-low-cost-high-impact.aspx.

77  Victor Lipman, "66% of Employees Would Quit if They Feel Unappreciated," *Forbes*, last modified April 15, 2017, https://www. forbes.com/sites/victorlipman/2017/04/15/66-of-employees-would-quit-if-they-feel-unappreciated/#276dda106897.

78  Ken Blanchard and Spencer Johnson, *The New One Minute Manager* (New York: HarperCollins Publishers, 2015).

79  Daniel Goleman, "What Makes a Leader?" in *On Leadership* (Boston: Harvard Business School Publishing, 2011).

80  Brent Schrotenboer, "Working at Home Had a Positive Effect on Productivity During the Pandemic, Survey Shows," *USA Today*, last modified June 2, 2020, https://www.usatoday.com/story/money/2020/05/04/coronavirus-pandemic-might-game-changer-working-home/3061862001/.

81  Schrotenboer.

82  "Leadership Podcast: The Six Types of Leaders, Part I," Life Church, accessed June 30, 2020, https://open.life.church/training/166-leadership-podcast-the-six-types-of-leaders-part-1.

83  Kristi Hedges, "How Are You Perceived at Work? Here's an Exercise to Find Out," *Harvard Business Review*, December 19, 2017, https://hbr.org/2017/12/how-are-you-perceived-at-work-heres-an-exercise-to-find-out.

84  "Coaching for Behavioral Change," Marshall Goldsmith, accessed June 30, 2020, https://marshallgoldsmith.com/articles/coaching-for-behavioral-change-2/.

85  "Teachers need real feedback," TED: Ideas Worth Spreading, May 2013, https://www.ted.com/talks/bill_gates_teachers_need_real_feedback.

86  "ICF Definition of Coaching," International Coach Federation, accessed June 30, 2020, https://coachfederation.org/about#:~:text=ICF%20defines%20coaching%20as%20partnering,their%20personal%20and%20professional%20potential.

87  "Introducing Rocky AI—Your Pocket Leadership Coach," Rocky, April 8, 2019, https://www.rocky.ai/post/introducing-rocky-ai-your-pocket-leadership-coach.

88  "HR Chatbot Executive Coach: Introducing LEADx Coach Amanda," accessed June 30, 2020, https://leadx.org/hr-ai-chatbot-coach/.

89  Chip Bell, "Learning as a Competitive Strategy," *ATD Insights* (blog), August 21, 2012, https://www.td.org/insights/learning-as-a-competitive-strategy.

90  Vanessa LoVerme Akhtar, "Leadership Lessons from Astronaut Scott Kelly," *Forbes*, March 2, 2016, https://www.forbes.com/sites/johnkotter/2016/03/03/leadership-lessons-from-astronaut-scott-kelly/#1febe1812d93.

91  Morgan McFall-Johnsen, "Elon Musk told NASA astronauts' kids ahead of SpaceX launch, 'We've done everything we can to make sure your dads come back OK,'" *Business Insider*, May 27, 2020, https://www.businessinsider.com/elon-musk-spacex-astronaut-families-launch-2020-5#:~:text=Elon%20Musk%20appeared%20to%20choke,your%20dads%20come%20back%20OK.%22.

92  Noel M. Tichy, *The Leadership Engine: How Winning Companies Build Leaders at Every Level* (New York: HarperCollins Publishers, 1997).

93 Jim Collins, *Good to Great: Why Some Companies Make the Leap... and Others Don't,* (New York: HarperCollins Publishers, 2001).

94 Kurt Lewin, Ronald Lippitt, and Ralph K. White, "Patterns of Aggressive Behavior in Experimentally Created Social Climates," *The Journal of Social Psychology 10*, No. 2, 269-299. doi:10.1080/002 24545.1939.9713366.

95 Ken Blanchard, Patricia Zigarmi, and Drea Zigarmi, *Leadership and the One Minute Manager* (New York: William Morrow and Company, 1985).